100 years of *Life* in our Church
1907-2007
The Story of Trinity-Henleaze United Reformed Church,
from the beginning.

Evelyn Bentley
Bert Bentley
Graham Chamberlain
Tracey Lewis
Peter Miller

Edited by Sonia Glass

First published in 2007

© Trinity-Henleaze United Reformed Church
www.trinityhenleazeurc.org.uk

ISBN 978-0-9555527-0-0

British Library Cataloguing-in-Publication Data
A catalogue record for this book is available from the British Library.

Published by Redcliffe Press Ltd, Bristol
Typeset by Harper Phototypesetters Ltd, Northampton
Cover design by Mark Cavanagh
Printed and bound by HSW Print, Tonypandy, Rhondda

CONTENTS

INTRODUCTION

When I was introduced as a candidate for the ministry here, in 2003, I was intrigued to meet a church with two strong, established historical pasts, that had recently taken the brave step of uniting to become one new congregation. The previous year had seen an approach from the congregation of Trinity United Reformed Church, which had already celebrated its centenary in its Cranbrook Road church building, with a request that the Henleaze United Reformed Church might consider the uniting of the two. The relationship progressed well during a time of ministerial vacancy for both, the Elders paying particular attention to the need to build the friendships that underpin a sense of belonging to one whole new church.

Uniting two congregations meant that there were more people, and among them, a sense of energy and movement. The atmosphere is positive, and the all-age, broad community that we are has room for new ideas and experiments as well as the cherishing of traditions and well known ways. The congregation is blessed with people from a great variety of walks of life with a rich store of skills and experience, and the faith that gathers us together is explored with generous attitudes of openness and acceptance. It is a great Church in which to be the Minister, as, it turns out, many of my predecessors will testify.

The idea of writing a history book for the centenary celebrations of this church in Henleaze was welcomed as an interesting challenge. Five members of the church offered their services for the project, some with long memories here and others 'relative' newcomers. The cupboard upstairs in the Church House held lots of dusty books and bits of paper, many bundled together with pieces of string. These provided a complete set of minute books from Deacons/Elders meetings and church meetings since the foundation of the church. So, the assembled group shared out the records and started to read of the hopes and decisions of our fore-bears in the faith. Minutes are a great place to start, but it soon became apparent that many of the 'stories' of life in this church were not captured in such official records.

Many people have been asked for their memories and recollections of life and events in the history of the church. The stories have been remembered and told, and in themselves have offered food for thought. In remembering what's gone before us we've found healthy roots, still growing, from which we often still gather fruit in our life together.

We are not professional researchers or writers and we've debated whether this book can be called an 'official history' of the church. It does not claim to be definitive but we do hope that in the pages that follow you'll enjoy the stories and recollections we've gathered and in them find inspiration for the ongoing challenge of Christian life. If there are stories we've missed, we hope that you'll remember them and tell them yourselves.

We, the writing group, are grateful to all the members of the church who have contributed by writing and telling the stories of this church and its life. In particular I am grateful to the people who have researched, written and coordinated this book: Peter Miller, Evelyn and Bert Bentley, Graham Chamberlain and Sonia Glass who has edited it. Their work has been a long journey in which much has been discovered, not least new friendships.

Tracey Lewis
May 2007

CHAPTER 1
THE EARLY YEARS 1903–27

Ministers:
Thomas Hammond 1903–14
Alan Gaunt 1914–17
Burford Hooke 1917–18
Sydney Cave 1918–20
Eric McNeill 1920–26

The first quarter of our church's century saw it through a transition from the confident optimism of the Edwardian era and women's suffrage, through the horror and disillusion of the Great War to the social turmoil of the General Strike and the beginning of the painful time of the Great Depression. The years 1914–1918 saw the tragic death on active service of many young men.

Beginnings in a Day School

On a cycle ride down Henleaze Lane, 'a picturesque road leading from the Downs to Filton, much used by carriage folk and cyclists', Mr George Hoskin-Wicks saw a property for sale. It had been a Roman Catholic Convent Day School.

Mr Hoskin-Wicks was a member of the Congregational Churches Extension Committee which, having been formed in 1899, met regularly at Redland Park Church to plan a programme of church building for the growing city of Bristol in the new century.

Originally Henleaze Congregational Church was to have been built on the junction between Kersteman Road and Cranbrook Road, but the Presbyterians were anxious to build on that site and it was agreed to transfer it to them.

The Day School building, on Henleaze Road, together with one rood and sixteen perches of adjoining land, was bought for £1522. A committee was then set up to turn the property into a chapel, school, classrooms and caretaker's residence.

After renovation and decoration the school building was officially opened on 2 June 1903 with a special ceremony. The fact that the land and buildings were free of debt, thanks to generous contributions from every

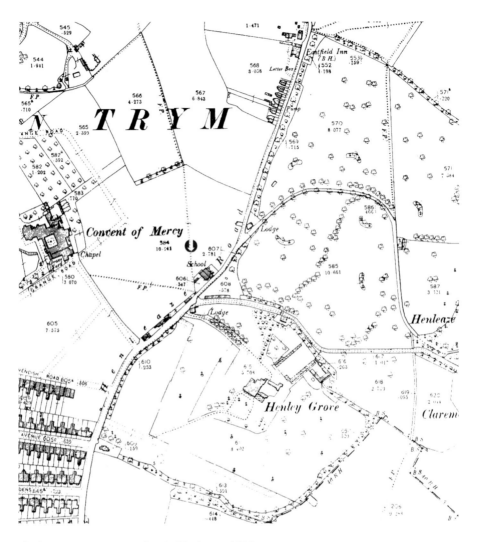

Ordnance survey map of early Henleaze, 1903

Congregational church in the city, was a matter of great celebration. The foundation of Henleaze Congregational church was said to be 'the most important thing Congregationalists have done in Bristol for 50 years.'

Services began in June 1903 and in September the building was registered as a place of worship. Discussions took place about holding morning services which many people wanted. However, it was felt that they could only hold evening services until the appointment of a Minister. The secretary to the sub-committee was David Laing, who became the first secretary of the Henleaze Congregational Church, and served in that capacity for 24 years. Reflecting on his period of service he was described as ' .. truly a living stone in the building.' He is remembered by a plaque in the church.

The Reverend Thomas Hammond, who had preached in Henleaze on 12 September 1903, was approached since he wanted to work in a smaller church than South Woodford where he was currently Minister. He was held in great esteem and was instrumental in the building of the new church. He, a man of private means, agreed to take up the appointment, with a stipend of £100 per annum, on condition that the finance was raised and the building of the church was started within the next two years.

In November 1903, the secretary David Laing invited Thomas Hammond to become Minister of Henleaze Congregational Church, 'In his hands it will prosper and be a power for great good in this district.' From then onwards things moved speedily forward.

It was soon apparent that the needs of the church would quickly outgrow this building, and attention was turned to the possibility of building a new church on the spare ground behind the original building. The architect, Mr Frank W. Wills – later Sir Frank Wills and a Lord Mayor of Bristol – was engaged for the design of the church. The accounts for 1907 show that the architect's fees were £248-8s. By 1905, a new building had been designed and tenders for the building work were obtained from

Memorial stones of David and Jeannie Laing

Henleaze Congregational Church, c. 1906 *(Samuel Loxton collection)*

eight contractors and the tender from G. Clark & Sons in the sum of £5,503 was accepted. When the work was started in late 1905, funding from various sources amounted to about £4,500 and the debt of £1,000 was not cleared until 1917.

The original design incorporated a spire on the tower at the south west corner of the building, and it is not clear from the records exactly when or why it was decided to omit the spire, leaving the tower as it is today with a flat roof.

In April 1906, the stone laying ceremony took place with the laying of four stones by prominent members of the Congregational Church in Bristol. The church building was ambitiously large because 'the building had to be ready for the neighbourhood as it developed and it was better to be in advance of the neighbourhood than the other way round.'

The buildings

On Saturday 28 April 1906, a special service was held to celebrate the laying of the corner stones, and by the end of 1906 the building was completed in time for the grand opening service on 9 January 1907. Also in time for the opening service was the delivery of 250 chairs at a cost of 3/4d each (just 17p in today's currency!).

According to our records, very few alterations were made to the church in the early years – hardwood panelling was added to the walls of the chancel in 1909 as a result of a donation from a 'friend of the church'. There had been an ongoing problem with the acoustics and in 1918 it had been remarked that the visiting preachers' sermons had been 'very helpful and well heard.' A variety of devices had already been tried to remedy the problem and these included putting a board above the pulpit and moving the pulpit around in different positions. The problem remained until 1919 when Professor A.M. Tyndall of Bristol University (their Great Hall had a similar problem) was approached and he suggested the installation of a 'complete false ceiling' comprised of a thick hessian type material at the level of the tie beams of the main roof trusses. However unsightly it was (and completely blocking out the lovely roof lining from view), this false ceiling must have been considered to be an advantage as it survived for the best part of 50 years until it was removed when electronic equipment was able to overcome such acoustical problems.

The new church building was furnished with chairs, not pews, because they were cheaper; saving £250. An envelope system was introduced for people's giving, rather than pew rent. The oak chairs were still in use in 1951 when discussions again took place about replacing them with pews. However, the cost of pews being £1216, after careful considerations it was decided to keep the chairs. By 1980 the rush seated chairs had developed 'a sinking feeling' when sat upon and so a 'cushion-making' party was mustered and set to work. Their work was overtaken, however, by the gift of new blue upholstered chairs from Audrey Venning who decided that the legacy she intended to make to the church should be given early while she could see and enjoy it with her friends.

The pulpit was made from ancient oak from the Froom Valley (Frome Valley) which had been the gathering place for Dissenters ejected from their meeting places in the seventeenth century.

Opening of the church

On 9 January 1907 Henleaze Congregational Church was opened by the Revd. C. Silvester Horne, a leading Congregationalist and member of Parliament. The ceremony was attended by the Lord Mayor and Lady Mayoress, and the High Sheriff, and tea was served in the school room at 5pm.

On 9 May 1907, a special meeting of members of the fellowship was held in the school room to pass two resolutions. The first one was to constitute the church and the second to agree a formula for electing deacons. The constitution called for the election of six male deacons. They were David Laing, Herbert Wheeler, E.P. Walker, Clifford Dixon, F.W. Thornley and W. Jeffrey. In 1916 two women deacons were added to the number, Mrs H.C. Leonard and Miss Collins, making Henleaze Congregational Church the first in Bristol to elect women deacons.

Some 50 people signed the role of membership under the words:

"We the undersigned being known to one another as believers in our Lord Jesus Christ and seeking to be his disciples hereby agree to unite together in forming ourselves into a Christian Church which will henceforth worship and hold its meetings in the Congregational Church at Henleaze."

9 May 1907

Aims of the new church

At the opening of the church the Revd. C. Silvester Horne, preaching on the spiritual power of sacred places said: 'Will you believe with me that our power in this place of Christian worship to convince and convert, to change the mind, to create faith where faith is not, and awaken love where love is asleep or even dead, our power to do these things depends not on this pulpit but on the reality of our worship, the intensity of our common faith and common prayer ...'

It was strongly felt that it should be a 'worship church' with real spiritual prayer and praise. Church meetings should be held monthly, on the last Wednesday of the month, and should not be just for administration, 'but for stimulating and guiding the spiritual life of the church, where each man can feel that they can make their contribution to church life.' They were concerned about work amongst young people in the Sunday School, out of which grew the Boy's Club in Westbury on Trym, working 'among rough working lads', since no other organisation provided for them.

Later, in 1913, the Revd. Hammond stressed the need for more of a social element in church life, so that members could get to know each other better.

Junior Church

From the earliest days there has been concern for young people. Our first minister, Thomas Hammond, began his ministry on 6 March 1904 and a Sunday School commenced on 10 April 1904 with 24 scholars and six teachers. During Sydney Cave's ministry, 1918–1920, it was agreed to hold a Dedication Service for teachers in the Sunday School in order to emphasise the witness of the church in the Sunday School. Dr Cave said 'that youth was the time for choice, four-fifths of the children passing through the Sunday School never joined the church'. A League of Young Worshippers was formed to link the children with the church. An innovative proposal came in 1924 during the ministry of Revd. Eric McNeil with the formation of a Hobbies Club for boys. Mr McNeil had trained as an engineer and was able to help them with the new-fangled wireless.

As early as 1907 there was a Boys' Club which met in the schoolroom with a large number attending the lantern service on Sunday evenings. A few years later a paper was read at a church meeting on 'work among the young and methods which would attract the scholars to the church and absorb them in church membership'. On one occasion a service of dedication was held for four new teachers to make them feel that they were doing great work and 'show that the church gave not merely money but workers and interest'. A paper dated 2 August 1916 and headed 'The church and young people' begins: 'It is unnecessary to labour the point of the importance of this subject. We will take it as accepted that it is a matter of vital importance'. An interesting further sentence reads, that 'much will depend upon the friendliness and constant interest shown by the minister in particular and also the deacons and members of the congregation generally in the young people individually'. It was also felt that a Catechism class for young people would help them.

By 1921 further proposals were made that:

1. Junior Church aged 12–14 were to be regarded as members but not to attend church meetings, vote on church affairs or take Communion.
2. Those aged 15–17 could take Communion but not vote until aged 21 when they had full church membership.

The Henleaze Church Sunday School's 18th annual report recorded that 'fourteen of our scholars recently sat for the scripture exam of the SLU, the result of which was received this morning and it is of a gratifying nature. In the first place all the candidates have been successful, four passing second class, eight first class and two in honours. Secondly, of the two in honours one has gained the fifth prize in the Bristol district, and one the first prize. Lastly, the school through these scholars has won the challenge shield given to the School which achieves the best result.'

Music: The organ

Minutes of meetings of 1907 record that a small positive organ, costing £100, was bought and that a doubtless hard-working individual was then engaged to operate its hand blower. A deacons' meeting minute of 1920 recalls that this instrument had been installed 'for temporary use'. It was evidently still serviceable after 13 years but was judged to be no longer adequate to support congregational singing. The organ was subsequently sold to Mangotsfield Congregational Church where, in October 1968, it was again to be played by a Henleaze church organist when our choir gave an evening concert of music at the church in Mangotsfield where it was still in good voice.

Discussion and fund raising in aid of a new organ began during the short ministry of Sydney Cave. A letter to church members reminded them that 'if the church is to do its full duty, it obviously must be efficiently equipped in every part of its services, and good music is becoming an increasingly important factor in making an appeal to the large numbers in all ranks of life who at first are but little attracted to religious services'. Thus, in 1921, the fine instrument was bought which, conserved and extended over the years, continues to serve our needs today. Built by J. G. Haskins & Co of Bristol for the sum of £778, the two-manual organ had seven ranks on great, seven on swell and three on pedal with couplers and composition pedals. Mr Morgan, the organist at St Mary Redcliffe, gave its opening recital. An electric blower was installed in 1924. The organ's tonal specification remained basically unaltered until recent times. The hand blower was kept and used as a reserve source of energy for the organ until the 1940s.

From the earliest years two members of the congregation, C. T. Joll and C. C. Hydes had served unpaid jointly as organist and choirmaster until, in 1923 under what are described as 'difficult and disheartening conditions', it was recommended with their agreement that there was a need for a single experienced leader, who would be paid, to serve as organist and to build up and train the choir. The deacons were concerned at that time that the church was 'failing to realise its mission' in attracting a fair proportion of newcomers to the district who were 'arriving everyday'. Uninspiring congregational singing was thought to be one reason for this failure and a committee had been appointed to consider 'how the congregational singing in the services of public worship in our church may be improved'. A. B. Hunt was appointed as our first salaried organist and choirmaster and thus began a period of professional leadership of music at Henleaze that was to last for over 50 years.

The church and its neighbours

Attendance at worship gave cause for concern and it was thought that it might help to introduce 'a more social element in the church life', and 'bring children into closer connection with the church'. So a Morning School was started to give children the opportunity to attend morning service, and a junior choir formed to supplement the main choir.

The Victorian attitude that children should be seen and not heard prevailed into the early 1920s. A request to 'find harmless recreation for young people who might otherwise go to questionable places' was met with the repost that 'it was not the real work of the church'. Children were denied the use of the school room for dancing classes while the tennis club could use it for a whist drive. There were complaints about those attending young people's parties: 'things were done that were very much out of place on church premises'. However, as the decade progressed a more tolerant attitude to children was adopted by the church; in 1925 the church started up an evening activity called 'Play House' for young children from the neighbourhood, once a week, and the Minister started a group for boys aged 11–15 years so that he could help and advise them on their hobbies.

The church had rooms and halls to offer to local people for their meetings and gatherings and as Henleaze grew as a residential area, different interest, social and other groups began to meet in the buildings; in the early 1920s, Badminton House Junior School used the school house hall for six weeks, and a Library Social Club, Literary and Social Club, Choral Society and Girl Guides group began to meet in the rooms available at the church.

Henleaze Church assisted in the community with representation on, and donations to, a Church Housing scheme instigated by The Council of Christian Churches, by which old properties in Bristol were restored and let to poor people at 10s per week.

Bazaars were organised in successive years to pay off large outstanding sums, which they did with great success. In 1927, a bazaar raised the grand total of £179 which enabled organ and heating system bills to be paid. The most ambitious plan in 1932 was to hold such a fundraising event over a three-day period to reduce debt on the Manse.

As the decade came to a close the Deacons opposed measures to grant licences for the sale of spirits, for the extension of licensing hours, and were against the growth of gambling. The Sunday opening of cinemas was an issue, especially as it reduced the attendance of young people at church. This was a period of expanding commitment to wider communal interests; permission was granted to use the church porch for taking of signatures in support of a petition against hunting of wild animals, for accepting money and clothing donations for the Miners' Distress Fund, and collections were also made for the rising numbers of unemployed.

Taking a pastoral interest in its members and neighbours, the church divided Henleaze into three areas each under the care of a lady deacon. These deacons would visit the sick and be on the lookout for new residents. They would advise the Minister when house calls were required. Some 2500 cards were distributed in the community advertising church services.

Ministers

Thomas Hammond resigned in 1914 owing to failing health and feeling that the church needed a younger man to carry on the work. Mrs Hammond was presented with a 'bag of gold' (£75), 'as a token of affectionate regard, and of the ideal way in which they had served the church.'

During the next five years the church was served by a number of Ministers including Allan Gaunt, who died suddenly following an operation; Burford Hook who served as a temporary Minister (during whose time the debt on the church building was paid off); and Sydney Cave, during whose ministry the problem with the acoustics was finally resolved.

Sydney Cave became Minister at Henleaze in April 1918, aged 34 years. It was to be his only local church ministry in this country. Trained at Hackney College under P.T. Forsyth, who regarded him as the best student that Hackney College had ever had, his desire had long been to serve as an overseas missionary. In 1908 the London Missionary Society appointed him to serve in South India. He came home on his first furlough leave in 1916, Mrs Cave having returned in 1914 with their children, and decided in the interest of the children's health, not to return.

Thus he came to Henleaze, and for the 1919–20 session also lectured at Western College, Bristol. His ministry at Henleaze was remembered with gratitude, his sermons deemed to be helpful and – importantly due to acoustic problems for the spoken word – he could be heard. It was a short ministry as in March 1920 he was called to be President of the Cheshunt

Thomas Hammond

Alan Gaunt

Burford Hook

Sydney Cave

11

College Cambridge, moving in 1933 to be Principal of New College London, a post which he held until his death in 1953. From 1936 he was Professor of Theology in London University.

Whether in charge of a congregation or in the training of Ministers, Sydney Cave is remembered as a fine teacher of the Christian faith and a caring pastor.

In 1920 Eric McNeill succeeded Sydney Cave as Minister of the church. During his ministry he introduced changes in the conduct of services which were not liked by everyone. Style and churchmanship were sensitive issues, 'Congregationalists were apt to cry "Popery" long before sight of a candle,' it was said. It was suggested at a Deacons' meeting that Deacons should be consulted about any changes before they happened, to which McNeill replied that it was up to him to arrange services. The matter was then brought up at a church meeting where after a long discussion it was resolved that the Deacons had to be consulted before any fundamental change. When they and the Minister had agreed a change, it would be referred to church meeting.

In 1921 it was proposed to hold a Hymn Singing service at the end of evening worship, that 'might attract some of the cottage folk in the district.' The following year the young people were asked to take part once a month in evening services.

By 1923, church attendances were growing and it was decided to set up a 'Look Out Committee' of six regular attenders sitting in different parts of the church, whose duty was to notice and welcome newcomers sitting near them and coming regularly and to report back to Deacons. Particularly they were to notice and welcome 'any shy or lonely young people and do their best to make them feel at home.'

Douglas Evans began a nine-year Ministry at Henleaze in 1927 which saw the celebration of a semi-jubilee the following year. At these celebrations the church made David Laing a Life Deacon, he and Mrs Laing being presented with a clock in recognition of their long service to Congregationalism in Bristol.

This was a time of considerable activity in the life of the church; 4 Park Grove was bought as a Manse for £925.00, using a bank loan, which was wiped out six years later by the holding of fundraising bazaars and gift days. New committees were formed, included one for publicity and a coordination committee; 2,500 cards were distributed in the area publicising a series of sermons; a joint canvas was held with the new St Peter's Church (built in 1927), and car lifts were offered to the elderly and infirm. Someone even suggested that they might have an early morning service to catch Lake bathers. A Young Worshippers League was formed to

Eric McNeill

look after children. A Men's Fellowship was started which met in members' houses until it was discontinued in 1956.

The years of Douglas Evans' Ministry were summed up in words that he used at a church meeting, that the theme of the church should be, 'Enthusiasm, Perseverance, Unity.'

CHAPTER 2
THE CHURCH IN A
GROWING COMMUNITY
1927–47

Ministers:
G. Douglas Evans 1927–36
W. Bramwell Jones 1937–55

This period saw our church through the depression of the 1930s, the Jarrow March, the Abdication, the Spanish Civil war, the rise of Nazi and Fascist tyrannies in Europe and finally the six years of the Second World War with further loss of life amongst young church members.

The church and its neighbours

In the late 1920s the church continued an advertising scheme in the growing local neighbourhood. Cards giving information about church services and inviting people to attend were distributed. New housing was being built in Henleaze and the church was keen to reach out to the new residents settling in the area.

In 1931 Henleaze Church took part in a 'Campaign of Youth', an effort to reach young people not attending any church.

In 1932 a further 2,000 invitation cards were distributed in the neighbourhood with the intention of reaching newcomers. These distributions increased over the next few years as more new houses were built. Indeed, well into the 1940s visiting cards were still being delivered to new residents, by which time the new housing consisted of the 'Grange Park Estate'.

In its relations with local groups meeting in the church halls and buildings a lively discussion about appropriate use continued. There was strong disapproval of the Henleaze Tennis club holding a Christmas Prize Draw on church premises.

The Choir organised Choir Festivals in 1931 and 1932. These were successful events which seem to have continued for some years.

There was a lively and active social conscience. From the church, money and clothing was collected and sent to the Miners' Distress Fund. There were collections also for the increasing number of unemployed and during the Second World War the church took steps to respond to the needs that presented themselves. They began to talk about providing crèche facilities for the local neighbourhood.

Into the 1940s a nightly canteen was opened on church premises for troops in the area, among them American soldiers who had been billeted in Henleaze. The arrival of Black American soldiers was something very new for Henleaze. The canteen was well-used, providing recreational activities, games, billiard table and a piano, and opportunities to talk or even pray with volunteers. The provision of the canteen, open every night, was appreciated by those whom it served but the noise it engendered could prove an unwelcome distraction at the times of Sunday worship. The soldiers often 'preferred to go into town on Saturday night' and efforts by the Deacons to encourage church attendance by the soldiers had limited success. In 1940 the women's circle started knitting helmets and socks for soldiers – and apparently little messages were put inside the socks.

Driven by the austerity of war, church premises were used more frequently for community purposes: for the distribution of gas masks, as a polling station, and for whist drives and private parties, one of which was a wedding reception. Before the war, harvest festival fruit and vegetables were sent to Southmead Hospital, but as Southmead now grew its own produce, it was decided to send donated food to 'voluntary' hospitals instead. Initially this meant that the Bristol Royal Infirmary became the recipient.

Terrill House, in Apsley Road, Clifton, was opened in the 1940s by the Bristol Free Church Housing Association, as a residential home for people over 60 years old. Over the years members from several churches, including Henleaze URC, helped with cleaning and cooking in the home and led services of worship. In the 1990s we had a member on the House Committee. The trustees have recently handed the property over to the MHAcare group, who will convert it into flats to be sold to selected elderly people.

The Reverend W. Bramwell Jones 1937–55

Bramwell Jones became Minister of Henleaze Congregational Church in 1937, and was the longest serving Minister the church has known. He was Minister during the Second World War and with his wife, Gwyneth, did much to guide the church in its service to the local community in wartime. Bramwell and Gwyneth, together a strong team, were a great blessing to

W. Bramwell Jones

the church in the difficult days of war and worked tremendously hard to provide an anchor for the church family at that time.

On the day war was declared in 1939, Bramwell had organised a Youth Service at Henleaze Congregational Church. Bramwell conducted the service and the address was given by a young man from the Bristol Itinerant Preachers Society, Cyril Grant. He became a Congregational minister in 1948 and is now a member of Trinity-Henleaze URC, in its centenary year.

Their encouragement and concern for young people in the church was something which is still remembered by many and no doubt resulted in these young people continuing with their involvement with the church in the years that followed.

Bramwell is remembered as an eloquent preacher and much loved pastor. Gwyneth, his wife, as a great organiser who encouraged the congregation's involvement in lots of communal activities. On Sunday evenings the youth group gathered at the Manse, having been to Morning service, afternoon Sunday School and Evening service. As early as 1937, a junior church membership scheme was introduced whereby children aged 14 to 16 became

Junior Members, young people aged 16 to 18 became Communicant Members and young people aged 18-plus became Full Members.

Bramwell was everybody's friend, helping local people with the problems that arose in war years. People of all ages came to respect him and his wife Gwyneth for their total dedication to their work in Henleaze. They had a great reputation for parties at the Manse. Gwyneth would organise a troop of volunteers to carry chairs and crockery from the church to Cavendish Road. She made wedding cakes for war time weddings in the church.

Bramwell was taken seriously ill during his ministry at Henleaze, taking nearly a year to recover. Gwyneth would keep a note board and pencil on the front door, suspended by a piece of string, on which a daily report of Bramwell's health would appear – and well wishers could write their greetings which would be taken in at the end of the day.

From Henleaze, Bramwell was called to his final ministry at Hoylake. On retirement he and Gwyneth returned to live in Henleaze. Within one year Bramwell died. Gwyneth took up a full and active role in the life of Henleaze URC, becoming an elder. Her service to the church over many years was recognised when she was appointed as an Elder Emeritus at her retirement. She continued in active membership until she died at the age of 100. On what would have been her 101st birthday the church held a

Ron and Moira Bocking, John and Majory Salsbury, Bernard and Brenda Chart, Gwyneth Bramwell Jones

service of thanksgiving for Gwyneth's life at which her daughter, Sheila, paid moving tribute to her mother.

The Second World War

By 1936 collections for the relief of refugees in Germany were being organised and the church regularly displayed posters inviting refugees in the locality to come along to church services and social activities.

The war affected the church in many ways – the shortage of coke for the boiler led to morning and evening worship often being uncomfortably cold and the near-proximity of the church to the Filton airfield made air-raid precautions a major concern; there was a worrying problem about having ladders long enough to reach the roof in order to tackle incendiary bombs, and where to locate the essential static water tank.

The church membership, in common with many families, had to endure the tragedies and privations of war. The names of those church members who tragically lost their lives on active service are recorded on tablets in the church dedicated to their memory. Each year, at the morning service on Remembrance Sunday, our children and young people still lay flowers at memorials.

Reflections on the Second World War and VE Day

Newsletter May 1995

Gwyneth Bramwell-Jones wrote:

The month of May sees the anniversary of our own VE Day, so celebrating the Allied victory in Europe. I have been asked to mark this historic anniversary by writing a resumé of how Henleaze celebrated the victory. It was a war that lasted six terrible years and the victory was only possible through the sacrifices of so many brave men and women in the country and Commonwealth. The church lost gallant young men: their names are remembered on the church war memorial.

My husband became a warden with the ARP (Air Raid Precautions). He was out nearly every night of the week patrolling the streets of one locality where the City of Bristol was blitzed and furiously burning. I joined the WVS and cooked breakfasts on rota for the wardens at Southmead Hospital who came off duty at 6.00am. Another activity I assisted with was help with the evacuation of Bristol children to the Lizard (Cornwall) by train from their various homes. It was a very sad occasion to see the parents saying 'goodbyes' and farewells at departure. I, too, felt for them as my daughter had gone to North Wales before leaving for Milton Mount college which had evacuated to Lynton from Sussex, we dearly missed her.

The church at Henleaze opened a canteen for the American soldiers billeted in the district. The canteen provided refreshments, card games, billiards, darts and piano music. Like so many people away from home, some soldiers were very homesick; they were so appreciative of the kindness shown to them by the men and women who manned the canteen each night.

When the cessation of hostilities had been announced my husband, Bramwell, conducted worship on the 8 May at 7.30 pm a service in the church. It was a very emotional service opening with the hymn 'Now thank we all our God'. It was a full church, there was hardly a dry eye at the close of the service, after the experience of so many years of assault bombing raids and food rationing.

The members of the young people's fellowship walked into town, where were a lot of people in the Centre, then walked up to Cabot Tower and they danced round the base. They returned up Whiteladies Road and home. Next day a picnic was arranged at the tennis club with a bonfire and fireworks.

Henleaze Road celebrated the victory with a street party provided by the shop proprietors on trestle tables. We had dancing and music and fireworks, with a large bonfire burning at the end of Cavendish Road opposite the Manse as it was then.

This is a very brief account of what took place. There were so many personal celebration parties but now I conclude with a short prayer –

That our young people will never endure the horrific experiences that the people who lived through the years 1939–45 came through. Sirens sounding every night, all running to their air raid shelters and staying until the all-clear was heard.
Yet again 'NOW THANK WE ALL OUR GOD'.

CHAPTER 3
THE DEVELOPING CHURCH
1947–67

Ministers:
W. Bramwell Jones 1937–55
D. Melville Jones 1956–62
Wilfred Salmon 1962–69

This post-war period saw great changes and the determination to re-build. The Welfare State, the development of the Commonwealth, the advance of Socialism, Suez and the Korean War, the Beatles and the 'Swinging Sixties'.

Mr and Mrs Hampden Leonard honoured

The post-war period saw an expansion of house building in Henleaze to which the church responded in specific ways. Earlier proposals to provide a crèche for the community were realised and the district circularised. Chess and badminton clubs were formed, and a car rota provided for those requiring transport to church. By way of entertainment Henleaze Congregational was beaten at cricket by St Peter's and the drama group was active.

In 1951 the church honoured Mr and Mrs Hampden C. Leonard, making them both Life Deacons in acknowledgement of their service to the church since 1908. Mr Leonard had been the church treasurer for many years, and Mrs Leonard (one of the first women to be elected a Deacon) had worked for many years with the Sunday School. The chairs on which the servers sit during communion services were given in memory of these two devoted servants.

Youth work

Pilots

In 1957 a 'Pilots' group, organised by the Congregational Union Churches for boys and girls 6–14 years, was set up at Henleaze. Pilots took part in recreational activities and learnt about the work of the London Missionary Society, in particular the John Williams Missionary ship. They went camping in the summer and in the winter used the hut at the back of the church in Henleaze Road for carpentry. This lively group of young people quickly gained a reputation, it being remarked that if there were any real problems in the church, it was 'always the fault of the Pilots'.

Cubs and Scouts

In 1958 there was already a Cub Pack at Henleaze, but no Scout Group, so on reaching scout age, the boys joined the Scout Group at St Peter's Church. However, in 1961, an experienced Scoutmaster, Tony Dyer, nephew of the church secretary J.M. Chamberlain, formed their own Scout Troop at the Congregational Church. On 3 December 1961 the newly formed Scout Group attended the morning church service for the presentation and blessing of the new Troop flag. The flag was placed on the table in front of the congregation before the service began. During the first hymn the colour party took their place in front of the table and the rest of the Troop formed up behind them. The Scouters and the District Commissioner took their places at the side. A short ceremony of blessing followed during which all the Scouts renewed their promise. The flag was handed to the Bearer and the National Anthem was played. The Troop, led by their new flag, marched in procession to the rear of the church.

The Scouts enjoyed a full and adventurous programme of activities. There are many stories of camp activities. Ian Cameron tells how, on his 24 hour hike, part of the course for graduating to Senior Scout, he, accompanied by Peter Bentley, camped overnight in a field from which they were chased by a herd of cows! The troop often gained 'excellent appraisals' from the District Commissioner.

Brownies and Guides

By 1954 there were two Brownie Packs meeting at the Congregational Church and one Guide Company which by 1960 had grown to become two companies. Rainbow Guides, for five to seven-year-olds started in 1992. Throughout the years many church members either helped lead or support the Brownie and Guide packs, which flourished over the years.

The Reverend Melville Jones 1956–62

Melville was the Minister of Henleaze Congregational Church when it celebrated its 50th Anniversary. He had become the Minister of the thriving church in 1956; membership stood at 227 which included fifty new members added during his first year.

The Jubilee Year Programme

Sunday 7 January 1957 at 6.30pm
COMMEMORATION SERVICE OF THE OPENING OF THE CHURCH on 9 January 1907

Thursday 14 March at 7.30pm
JUBILEE PARTY for surnames A to H

Thursday 11 April at 7.30pm
JUBILEE PARTY for surnames I to W

Saturday 4 May
10am–1pm and 2pm–5pm
The Minister will be pleased to receive gifts in the Vestry for the New Church Hall.

Sunday 5 May
JUBILEE SUNDAY
10.30am Prayer Meeting
Services at 11 am and 6.30pm will be conducted by:
The Reverend Howard S. Stanley M.A.
Secretary of the Congregational Union of England and Wales
Assisted by:
Revd. D. Melville Jones B.A. B.D.
The evening service will be attended by
The Lord Mayor and Lady Mayoress and the Sheriff and his Lady

Monday 6 May at 5pm
RE-UNION TEA
For past and present members and Friends
Greetings from representatives of local churches and Associations.
This function will be held at St Peter's Hall, the Drive.
All other events on our own premises.

At 7pm <small>A PUBLIC MEETING</small>
Theme: Past, Present and Future.
Chairman: Mr John M. Chamberlain
Church Secretary
Speakers: Mr Hampden C. Leonard
Revd. G. Douglas Evans
Revd. W. Bramwell Jones
Revd. D. Melville Jones

Thursday 9 May at 7.30pm
<small>JUBILEE CONCERT</small>
Clifford Harker
Organist of Bristol Cathedral
String Orchestra
Leader: Edwin Brown, leader of the Cathedral Orchestra
Soloists: Miss Edna Bennett
Mr Frank Boxall
The Church Choir
Organist and Choirmaster: Mr Roy Bradford

Summer
<small>THE CHILDREN CELEBRATE</small>

Autumn
<small>A CHURCH PARTY</small>

Jubilee Year 1957: John M. Chamberlain, Hampden C. Leonard, Douglas Evans,
D. Melville Jones, W. Bramwell Jones

The new church hall

The piece of land between the church and the first house in Waterford Road had remained vacant for 50 years since the church was built. It had not been wasted space as during the Second World War the caretaker had grown fruit and vegetables there and shared the produce with the neighbours. In the 1950s, following much debate, it was decided to build a new hall on the site and one of the church members, who was an architect, was commissioned to design the building. It was completed in November 1958 at a cost of a little over £5,000. This hall, known originally as the Large Hall and then later as the Waterford Hall, has served us well for 50 years.

Sunday School becomes Family Church

In 1958, after two years' discussion, the Sunday School leaders finally agreed to replace afternoon Sunday School with Family Church. This was divided into Children's Church (for those aged ten and under) and Junior Church (aged 11-15), and took place during the Sunday morning service. At the time it was said that, 'Those children who sat with their parents waited with eager anticipation to leave for their service.'

The change was quite momentous; it marked the beginnings of integrating children into the life of the whole church and indications of a changing attitude to children and family life in the wider society.

The great day came on 2 November 1958 when all the young people in church proceeded to the New Hall where they were split into age groups and departments. Each child was presented with a 'star card'. This was a membership card for all who had previously attended Sunday School.

A number of church members had worked for many years with the Sunday School, including Elvira Morris and her brother Leslie, and May Hemmons, affectionately known as 'Auntie May', who had been associated with the Sunday School since the beginning.

In 1961 Mr Melville Jones accepted the post of organiser of School Religion in Norfolk, and so left Henleaze. He took the post because he 'wanted to help to form children's ideas before they left school'. Church members at Henleaze were sorry to see him go and expressed their appreciation of his 'excellent work during his stay at Henleaze'.

Ladies' outing. "Auntie May" is in the striped dress

Women's meetings

Women's Circle

A knitting party was formed in the 1940s, when a small group of ladies met in each other's homes, sat in a circle, knitting and chatting. Their aims were both social and to raise funds for the church. In 1949, the weekly subscription was 2/- (10p), which was used to buy materials. Knitting soon expanded to include sewing and craftwork, everyone making items to sell at the 'sale of work' before Christmas. Later a cake stall was added to the sale.

The group became known as the Women's Circle, and an evening meeting was introduced for younger ladies with families or a job. Social activities included coach trips and an annual theatre trip (still taking place in 2006). Jumble sales were held regularly to boost funds, until the recent growth of charity shops. The Women's Circle continued to meet until 1964, since when, only evening meetings were held (as now) and the Ladies Guild was born in 1968.

Mrs Melville Jones set up a Young Wives Group as distinct from the afternoon Working Party. As time went by its members were faced with the problem of determining when a Young Wife was no longer 'young'. They resolved this dilemma by renaming their group the Evening Working Party and continued their monthly meetings in members' homes. They were an

We are amused

Audrey Venning, as Queen Victoria, with her young helpers

active group who contributed greatly to the life of the church undertaking duties in the church such as, cleaning, catering, flower arranging, curtain making and provided 'comfort and strength to one another in difficult times'. They raised a lot of money for the church and charities, eventually running the Annual Morning Market.

The Evening Working Party was finally disbanded in 2005, although today its six remaining members still meet in each other's houses.

Beryl Jack, long time member of the Evening Working Party, wrote:

The Evening Working Party HURC was started during Melville Jones' ministry when we were a fairly large group of young women. Over the years we very gradually lost members, mostly due to old age or by moving from the district, but we only actually disbanded last year, 2005. The six remaining members continue to meet once a month in each other's homes, as we have done for so long. It was always so very well supported by our families and friends in the church who also helped us a great deal in many ways. Most of us were also in the Drama Group where we all so enjoyed each other's company, from the older members down to the youngsters who liked being part of the group and were encouraged to take part in the activities. A very happy time was enjoyed by us all.

Ladies Guild

The Ladies Guild began in 1931 as the Women's Circle. It attracted church members and local residents to its Monday evening meetings to hear speakers, see demonstrations, hear concerts and take part in charity efforts. At the time there was also a large men's Fellowship in the church.

A very long serving member of the church, and President of the Women's Circle, was Mrs Gwyneth Bramwell Jones, whose husband was Minister for 18 years. Their garden at the Manse apparently contained a cage of 50 budgerigars, 5 hens, a white rabbit and 2 bee hives. Honey from the hives was sold, at the Ladies Guild, in aid of the London Missionary Society. Gwyneth gave the address at the 70th Anniversary celebrations of the Ladies Guild, as it had then been renamed, recounting her war time experiences. She spoke of the day she was asked to conduct the Women's World Day of Prayer service in Bristol Cathedral, with a vast congregation, all praying for peace.

The Ladies Guild has continued to thrive with between 45 and 60 members at any one time. They still meet fortnightly between September and May and have a fascinating range of speakers each year; one of the highlights being Cyril Grant's hilarious sideways looks at life!

An Away Day at Wesley College, with Cyril Grant lying on the floor!

The Morning Market

The Morning Market was a great event in the church's calendar. The arrangements were in the capable hands of the members of the Evening Working Party.

The Waterford Hall became a scene of great activity, with a large rectangle in front of the kitchen cordoned off for coffee and lunch, the remaining space around the hall filled with stalls offering exciting gifts, and a large rectangular stall down the centre of the hall filled with goodies for children, run by Junior Church. Every organisation in church was involved. On sale was jewellery, toiletries, books, beautiful embroidery, bric-a-brac and a Christmas cake given to the lucky winner who came nearest to guessing its weight. There was a bottle stall, run by the men, with each bottle marked underneath with a number, so one might be lucky enough to win a bottle of sherry with the number one had purchased, three tickets for a pound, or a bottle of HP sauce!

Sometimes there was a stall manned by the charity for that year, which provided publicity for that charity, with the takings made up to £200 by the church. Many different charities, the Home Farm Trust, Alzheimer's

Getting ready for market

Stallholders who wore costume at the Winter Wonderland market in Henleaze United Reformed Church. Adjusting their bonnets in the picture are, left to right, Mrs Joan Tankins, Mrs Joan Hubball and Mrs Phyliss Cole.

A newspaper cutting about the Morning Market

All dressed up for the Morning Market

Society, St Christopher's School, Claremont School, Abbeyfield were the beneficiaries of a gift from the church whether or not they had goods for sale from their stall. The Market would be opened by a speaker from the charity of the year or by the Minister.

Sometimes there was a special theme – naval, Scottish or a Welsh theme for example – with the stallholders appropriately dressed.

Many people from the neighbourhood visited the market, and it was well worth all the effort put into it.

Drama

The Drama Group began in the 1960s and was very popular, their productions being enjoyed by performers and audience alike. The highlights included *When we are married* by J.B. Priestley, *Dear Octopus* by Dodie Smith, *He that shall come*, by Dorothy L. Sayers, which involved almost the entire church family, and of course, the *Singing Dancing Carpenter* (mentioned elsewhere). A Sunday morning service was devoted to the production *Jonah – Man – Jazz*, a musical production of the Book of Jonah. This biblical story was first read in church in its entirety by Cyril Grant.

Music

Cleaning and overhaul of the organ in 1951 involved some re-voicing and the provision of a balanced swell pedal.

The golden age of choral music in our church was the long period from the late forties to the early seventies during which Roy Bradford was organist and choirmaster. Worship benefited, with a full contribution by the choir each Sunday morning through sung responses and the Lord's Prayer, a chanted psalm and an anthem, carefully prepared at Friday evening choir practice. Festivals were more often than not celebrated with a major choral work, most notably on each Palm Sunday. The choir had a professional soprano, Edna Bennett, as leader who served for over 25 years. The quality of the choir's singing can still be appreciated if one listens to the recording of its favourite pieces made in 1968. Moreover, the choir played a full part in the musical life of the city and district, regularly giving recitals by invitation at local churches. The esteem in which it was held in the Bristol musical establishment is exemplified by the fact that at a concert in the church to celebrate the jubilee of 1957 the choir was accompanied by a professional orchestra and by the organist of Bristol Cathedral.

Links with New Kingsland, Henbury United Reformed Church

As long ago as the 1960s the Congregational Church in Henbury asked if several families from our church would be willing to form the nucleus of a church in Henbury. They felt that other churches on the Henbury Estate were flourishing but the Congregational Church was moving backward rather than forward. Records do not show if anything came of the idea at the time but at a later date our church provided a church secretary, Sunday School staff and committee members for the Henbury Congregational Church.

In 2006 an appeal for help was made once again and another attempt to help this small church in its struggle for survival was launched; as was the case in 1960, it is without a Minister. Its membership of ten meet in a large hall built originally to be the Sunday School, on a large piece of land which has become unmanageable for the ageing membership.

Elders and Members from Trinity-Henleaze URC have attended services and church meetings at New Kingsland URC, provided musicians, and visited an Open Gardens Day in the delightful cottage garden of one of the members – in pouring rain! – always receiving a very warm welcome. In the autumn of 2006 members of New Kingsland attended the Harvest service at Trinity-Henleaze, and the monthly newsletter gives details of services at the Henbury Church and contact numbers for their secretary.

The Trinity-Henleaze Minister, together with a retired Minister and Elders, are continuing to support New Kingsland Church with the policy described in 1960 as 'planned good neighbours'.

CHAPTER 4
DIFFICULT TIMES FOR
CHURCH AND NATION
1967–87

Ministers:
Wilfred Salmon 1962-69
Ronald Batt 1969–76
Fred Pope 1976–77
Ronald Bocking 1978–88

These years saw Britain join the European Community. Americans landed on the moon, Britain experienced rising unemployment, high inflation, the winter of discontent and the three-day working week. The conflict with the IRA brought violence to the cities. There was war again in the Falklands conflict.

The Reverend Wilfred Salmon 1962–69

Early in Reverend Salmon's ministry, young mums were invited to meet at the Manse and this soon became a regular gathering. Similarly the young people in the church were invited to the Manse and requested that monthly meetings were held there after the Evening Services. In 1967 an evening worship was arranged and conducted by the young people and was felt to be so successful that it was decided to hold more in the future, perhaps quarterly.

The church widened its involvement in the life of the Henleaze neighbourhood when volunteers provided car lifts to church for elderly people and took part in a scheme developed by Bristol Old People's Welfare to take housebound people out for a drive. Volunteers were also asked to join with other local churches in a road warden's scheme. In 1962 a coffee morning was held for retired people and proved so popular that it was decided to hold it monthly. At the present time, there is a popular weekly Friday coffee morning where people call in and are welcome to join the Friday Prayer meeting.

Wilfred Salmon

The United Reformed Church

The most significant milestone for our church during its century – its foundation apart – was the change that occurred in 1972 when Henleaze Congregational Church became a member of the United Reformed Church.

In 1945 the Congregational Union of England and Wales and the Presbyterian Church of England set up a joint committee to consider the possibility of organic union. Discussions following this initiative continued until 1948 when it was finally concluded that a formal union was not acceptable.

The next significant move occurred in 1966 when our denomination agreed, by vote in Assembly, to change from the Congregational Union (of independent churches) to the Congregational Church in England and Wales. This fundamental change in structure thus predated the union with the Presbyterians by a period of only six years. It undoubtedly facilitated a union of mainstream Congregationalism with the Presbyterians but, at the same time, led finally to the secession of those churches of the

Congregational Union for whom independence was a non-negotiable principle and tradition.

Formal discussions with the Presbyterians had resumed in 1963 and the two churches united in 1972 to form the United Reformed Church. One reason, among many, for this step – said to be the first significant union of two Christian denominations in England since the Reformation – was disappointment and restlessness felt by many churchgoing Christians in this country at the seeming failure of the established and the free churches to make any significant progress towards formal union. In our neighbourhood this disappointment was countered by an increased determination by all the local churches to work together in ecumenical amity, an expression of local 'unity' that continues unchanged to this day through what was first styled the Westbury Council of Churches.

In 1972 each individual congregation, at a church meeting, had to decide whether or not to unite in the new church. The great majority of churches in our denomination decided to unite; some opted to continue to remain independent in a continuing Congregational tradition. At Henleaze we welcomed the union and soon became accustomed to the new experience of being governed by synod, perhaps most notably at the times of a ministerial vacancy. Reappointing Deacons, elected for a three year-term, automatically as Elders ordained for life, was more controversial and occasioned some spirited debate among those in our church family who were directly concerned.

Thereby our church at Henleaze left behind its rich heritage in the Congregational tradition in order to become an enthusiastic member of a new nonconformist reformed church. We had changed not just our name but, by the grace of God, our affiliation and system of governance as part of our continuing membership of the Church Universal.

It was agreed that each church should give up some 'cherished ideas and practice in the interests of unity'. The title Reformed Church was not generally liked, but they were 'unable to come up with a better name'. The general criticism was expressed that 'the Basis of Union gives the impression of having been written by a Presbyterian rather than a Congregationalist'. There were 3,000 Congregational Churches and 300 Presbyterian churches, with membership of 200,000 and 70,000 respectively.

The Reverend Ron Batt 1969–1976

In 1970, new members to the church found that it was so full that they had to be early to get a seat – and really early for the candle-lit service at

Ron Batt

Christmas. In fact, Henleaze Congregational Church, at this time, has been described as the 'fastest growing church in the South West'.

Ron Batt's early ministry was a time of great activity. A Pastoral Committee was set up to visit church families and Deacons were to visit church organisations. In 1970 sermons started to be recorded for those unable to get to church. For six years the Junior Church undertook responsibility for the health and education of Cecilia Siswas, an orphan in Calcutta. They raised the £36 needed each year by fundraising activities and contributions from their pocket money.

The Manse at 6 Owen Grove was bought for £7,250.

Luncheon Club

In the 1970s Ron Batt's concern for the social needs of elderly and retired people led him to look into the provision of a weekly luncheon club meeting in the Waterford Hall and the Old People's Welfare Luncheon Club opened in 1971. The city council delivered the food as our own cooking facilities were inadequate. Church members travelled around the Southmead estate in a council van, collecting club members, and 'Granny Bull' organised coffee on arrival, lunch and a cup of tea before they left. After a few years the city council pulled out of the catering arrangements. Church members tried to replace this service by cooking at home, but the club closed.

The long service to the church of several members was acknowledged in 1972 when John Chamberlain and Eric Smith were each presented with inscribed silver plates. In the following year the church secretary presented two Communion Plates in memory of Philip Greenwood who had been Church Treasurer for many years and had died in office.

In 1973 Paul Quilter, who had been a Junior Church leader was accepted for training for the Ministry.

The highlight of 1976 was the recording and broadcasting of the BBC Songs of Praise programme at our church.

An interesting innovation was the introduction of women door stewards, when wives were invited to join their husbands on door duty.

An aspect of church life which gave cause for concern was the poor attendance at church meetings. At the church meeting to discuss this decline it was suggested that the church was 'so governed by Elders who took the decisions' that church meetings had little point. So the format was changed to include group discussion and reporting back.

This lively church was over shadowed by the tensions over differing beliefs about the order and form of worship which came to be known as 'the troubles.'

During the time of the Reverend Ron Batt

These were difficult times. Worship, as the founding members of the Henleaze Congregational Church had hoped, was the strong core of church life from which all else flowed and great care and attention was given to the shape and quality of services in the church. Since the 1930s there had been much discussion in the wider Congregational movement about the proper form and characteristics of worship within the 'Reformed' tradition in which Congregationalism had its roots. Congregational worship had largely developed with the sermon as its central focus with the rest of the service described as 'preliminaries'. In many churches a sense of 'good order' had grown – some people feeling that services often leant too far towards a formal, almost Anglican, liturgical ethos. The Church Order Group, a national Congregational Union body, argued for more of a Reformed ethos for worship.

Over the previous years, when Wilfred Salmon and Melville Jones had been ministers, the debates over the form and style of worship had gathered some tension around them and opinions differed within the Henleaze Church locally. During the ministry of Ron Batt, in the early years of the United Reformed Church, some of the tensions involved in such discussions about worship were lived out and came to a head within the congregation at Henleaze.

Henleaze United Reformed Church was highly regarded in its reputation of excellent church music. Roy Bradford, the Organist and Choirmaster, and the accomplished choir, would participate in worship every Sunday morning with an anthem, sung responses and singing the Lord's Prayer. Both organist and choir took great pleasure in producing a very high standard of music to contribute to worship. Such was their ability that they made recordings and BBC broadcasts. The choir and musicians were an influential part of the church.

The choir's contribution was well established and strong and the organist resistant to change. The Minister, influenced by the Church Order Group's work, wanted to see changes in the conduct and traditions of worship; both were trying to hold on to the good things that were precious to them. Another point of contention was the extent to which money should be spent on upgrading the organ in relation to other spending priorities. Eventually the tension between the Organist and the Minister grew beyond an ability to resolve their differences. In 1974 Roy Bradford was required to leave.

Many members of the choir were deeply hurt in this breakdown of relationships and, in solidarity with the organist, the choir left the church. Almost one third of the church members also left in these troubled times.

The local press reported the story of these fractures within the church in ways that were very hurtful. The reasons for the organist and choir's departure were difficult to explain to the outside world and many were further hurt by the reported, groundless, suggestions of misdemeanours.

These difficult events left the church with a great sense of regret and sadness.

Worship changed rapidly after these events. Immediately following the resignation of the choir, members of the congregation responded to an invitation by the Minister to occupy the empty choir stalls to lead the hymn singing. Dr John Bishop was subsequently appointed Organist and Choirmaster, a position he held until after the beginning of the Ministry of Fred Pope.

During the interregnum between the ministries of Ron Batt and Fred Pope, the Elders wrote a carefully worded letter to every member who had left, asking them to consider a new beginning with a new Minister after these unfortunate events. They were invited to return if they so wished.

Playgroup

The Henleaze United Reformed Church Playgroup, located in the hall, opened in 1976. It was the idea of Judy Harris, a church member, who became its first leader.

The playgroup originally opened for four mornings a week, but as numbers declined, this was reduced to two mornings. Despite support from the church, which reduced the rental, its financial position was precarious, and at times it was difficult to buy paints, paper, etc. By 2000 it became clear that the playgroup could no longer survive in the changing educational climate when children were starting school at the age of four and there was more widely available child care for the under fours.

A lunch was arranged for the leaders and helpers who had given time, skill and enthusiasm to the playgroup and the leader and her assistant were each presented with a cheque from the church. The equipment was distributed to various other groups including Mothers and Toddlers, the Contact Centre and Junior Church.

Playgroup Christmas Party

The Reverend Fred Pope September 1976 – July 1977

Fred Pope, his wife and young family were happily settled in a church in Ware, Hertfordshire, when he was approached by the Moderators to fill the vacancy at Henleaze Congregational Church. The church was in turmoil, following the events referred to above.

Fred Pope was told by the Moderators that he was the ideal person to fill the vacancy since he was young enough to have the necessary energy as well as experience to offer. Although unhappy to leave the church in Ware he decided to accept the call. He visited his doctor for a health check and was told he was fit.

After visiting Henleaze to 'preach with a view', he felt called to lead worship there, and accepted the invitation to be the Minister. He set himself the task of a 'healing ministry'. To this end he invited groups of church members to coffee evenings at the Manse (6 Owen Grove) and was available at the Manse on Monday evenings and one morning a week in church for personal callers. This resulted in many church members crossing the Manse threshold for the first time. A number of those

Fred Pope

members who had left the church also went to see him to give him their viewpoint. He visited church members widely.

Ecumenical links with St Peter's were strengthened when it was discovered that Janet Cousins and Rose Pope had been friends at college.

After a brief nine months ministry, Fred Pope became ill and was diagnosed with Hodgkins Disease. The church members supported the family with many offers of baby-sitting and companionship. But sadly, after this brief nine months healing and pastoral ministry, Fred died in July 1977.

The 70th anniversary of the founding of the church fell during the interregnum, and it was decided to celebrate with a neighbourhood festival, in May 1978.

70th Anniversary – Neighbourhood Festival

The festival began with supper provided by the Young Wives Group attired in Edwardian dress. A pageant followed, introduced by the 'Recorder of Events' with many passages from the history of Bristol, including an authentically red-haired Queen Elizabeth and William Canynge. The pageant

Queen Elizabeth I and William Canynge (Kate Chamberlain and David Sheryn)

41

was followed by an Edwardian Music Hall with popular songs from that era.

The opening ceremony was performed by HTV newscaster Bruce Hockin, who invited everyone to come to the exhibitions which included paintings, pottery, photographs, calligraphy, the work of schools, Guides, Brownies, Junior Church and playgroups.

On Friday evening the church was full for a concert given by the Cotham School orchestra, the church organist David Old, and the Fairfield Singers.

On Sunday the church was full to capacity for the Reunion Service, conducted by the Reverend Basil Sims, when many old friends travelled to be with us. The evening service was conducted by Harold Sylvester and Edmund Shaw, with solos from Joan Yeadon and anthems by the choir.

Phyllis Cole, the church secretary wrote:

> It was with great joy that we received the news that Revd. Ronald Bocking had accepted the call to become Minister at Henleaze. This news, coming at this time, was indeed a fine climax to a wonderful weekend. In his letter to us Mr Bocking said that he felt this call came from God and that he looked forward to working with us all at Henleaze. Let us now be thankful to God for His guidance and pledge ourselves to working together in the time ahead for the good of our church and the community at home and abroad.

The Reverend Ronald Bocking 1978–88

In 1976 Henleaze Congregational Church made its first approach to Ronald Bocking, with the request that he consider becoming their Minister. However, owing to the ill-health of his colleague in team ministry in Harrow, he was unable to consider a move of pastorate at that time.

In 1978, after the unfortunately short Ministry of Fred Pope, the Elders again approached Ron with the request that he consider becoming Minister at Henleaze. Meeting to discuss the proposal, Ron listened as the church secretaries, Cliff and Phylis Cole, and the Elders told the story of the past few turbulent years. The 'troubles' the church had experienced were spoken of with a great sense of sadness, and a recognition of the healing pastoral ministry that Fred Pope had given to the church. Ron asked the Elders, 'What do you need a Minister for?' to which they replied, 'To help us develop a Christian understanding of church life.' He accepted the invitation to be their Minister.

Ron Bocking

Ron, with his wife Moira, moved to Bristol in 1978. The Revd. R.J. (Dick) Hall, the then Thames North Synod Moderator, preached the charge to church and minister at the Induction service.

In the weeks and months that followed, as Ron became familiar with the church, he realised the depth of pain that still surrounded the recent history of fracture in the church membership. The first two Elders meetings were held at the church, where Ron found many Elders to be reticent about speaking up. They were then invited to meet at the Manse where conversation was found to improve. They agreed that initial priorities had to be caring for the members of the church and establishing a period of stability in church life, within which it was hoped that healing could occur. They also agreed that encouraging the involvement of children should be a focus for the church and ministry.

Celebrating his first Christmas in Henleaze, Ron invited the children to be involved in planning and leading services. They took part with enthusiasm, suggesting all new hymns for singing. Ron advised a more measured approach with the combining of old and new as the way forward to a truly 'all age' approach. In subsequent years the church became an increasingly integrated community with people of all ages sharing festival services – the under 8-year-olds often returning to the service during the Offertory hymn to display their morning's work and creations.

The first four years of Ron's ministry saw no growth in the numbers of people attending the church – 19 church members died during his first six months – but then, slowly, new people started to attend and the congregation began to grow. One family came to the church one Easter Day because they had seen Ron Bocking's name on the noticeboard outside; Vic Cobley had served in the Army with Ron and had been impressed by Ron's attention to his prayers each night. He came to the church, renewed a friendship, and the family became long standing members.

Telephone Prayer Fellowship

There were several new initiatives within the life of the church, one of which, in the 1980s, was the Telephone Prayer Fellowship, to which all members of the congregation are invited to belong.

This Fellowship is a ministry where members will pray for anyone who may need support for whatever reason, be it bereavement, sudden illness, surgery, or facing a difficult decision in their life. Names of people for whom we are asked to pray, and which are confidential within the Fellowship, are passed on to each member by telephone, so a chain of prayer is quickly put in motion. We sometimes hear from those for whom our prayers have been requested, telling us how they have been strengthened and comforted by the knowledge that prayers have been offered for them.

Poetry Group

In 1986 the Poetry Group started at the home of Daphne Bloomfield. Members interested in poetry gathered once a month, to share the poems they had found on a chosen theme – or sometimes written themselves. Over the years many poems, and the personal stories and memories behind their choosing, have been shared in the very convivial company of the poetry group. To the present day, the group still meets on the last Tuesday of the month.

Henleaze Community Care Project

In the 1980s the Henleaze Community Care Project was launched under the auspices of the Bristol Churches Community programme. It was a joint project with St Peter's Church. It had two key aims: to provide employment for young people, especially girls for whom there was no existing employment programme in Bristol, and to fill the gaps in the care services met by the statutory body. After two years there was a staff of nine young people and two adults regularly visiting some 60 clients. Tasks included reading to partially-sighted people, preparing meals, cleaning, ironing, shopping and helping mentally handicapped people and those recovering from illness. When the Government ended the funding for this project all those young people still on the programme either obtained work in care homes or went into training for work with the elderly, with the exception of one young man who joined a circus!

Children's Holiday Clubs 1981–85

The Holiday Club was organised by Ron and Moira Bocking. It was open to all children in Henleaze between the ages of 5 and 12 for five mornings during the last week of August. The children were involved in painting, making models of Henleaze Road which included recognisable garden shop, Esso Garage, Barclays Bank and Aimee's, the fish and chip shop.

Ron Bocking with members of the Junior Church, at his retirement

They also learned first aid, knitting and bicycle maintenance and made music on hand-held chimes and xylophone with piano accompaniment.

Holiday Club had a serious objective, each day beginning with the singing of choruses and showing of cartoon film strip stories from the life of Jesus together with a memory verse text. Over 50 children enrolled on the first day and numbers grew during the week as the news spread. It was an important exercise in outreach.

Music

The organist, David Old's work commitments had become greater and he decided to retire from his duties at the church. Bert Bentley then took over at the organ, on a temporary basis that lasted 20 years. During this time, in 1980, Margaret Knoweldon joined the church. Soon after arriving she approached Ron Bocking offering to help out in the church. Ron suggested adding her name to the 'coffee rota', but after a few weeks it became evident that this was not where her talents lay. She offered to do something to do with music and the choir on the condition that the choir members wanted her to. It took the choir less than a minute to say 'Yes please!' and Margaret became the Choir Mistress. She exercised her considerable talents in this role for the next 24 years. Along with James and Jennifer Richards, her friends and fellow musicians, Margaret brought a considerable love and breadth of music to the life of the church.

In 2001 Clare Alsop was appointed as our first professional organist for over 20 years.

75th Anniversary of the church

The celebration of the 75th Anniversary of the church took place on the weekend of the 9 May 1982. Present at those celebrations were three ladies who, as children, had attended the laying of the church foundation stone ceremonies in 1906. They were Mrs Overton and Mrs Brooks who were sisters, and Mrs Chamberlain, who had attended the stone laying with her aunt and remembered being told to 'hold on to her penny.'

The Minister contacted Henleaze Junior School and asked if the children would like to do a local history project on the anniversary. The result was 'The History of Henleaze' performed by the children of the school, which included drawings, readings and slides of their activities.

There was also a Barn Dance organised by leaders of the Uniformed Organisations.

The highlight of the celebrations was the morning service, which included a baptism; many church members took part and the flowers were provided by the different organisations who each arranged a basket of flowers.

In the afternoon there was a tea party to which members from Wrington United Reformed Church (1662) and Dursley Tabernacle (1710) were invited. They were joined by friends from St Peters' Church and the Westbury Council of Churches.

The Songs of Praise evening service saw eight members of the church, each representing a decade in its history, invited to select three hymns from which one was finally chosen. Harold Sylvester then interviewed these members 'sympathetically' eliciting reasons for their choice. Mrs Brooks, representing the decade of the 1920s, was invited to choose the first hymn.

Evening Service Songs of Praise
6.30pm Sunday 9 May 1982

Notices

Introduction –
Wrington (1662) & Dursley Tabernacle (1710), long preceded Henleaze.

Prayer

Mr Harold Sylvester will talk with the representatives who have chosen the Hymns

1929	Mrs Alleyne Brooks	The King of Love my Shepherd is
1920–30	Mrs Irene Moore	All things bright and beautiful
1930–40	Mr John Chamberlain	Lord of all hopefulness
1940–50	Mrs Gwyneth Bramwell Jones	Jesus shall reign where ere the sun
1950–60	Mr Kenneth Meyer	When I survey the wondrous cross

Organ Interlude

1960–70	Mr Kenneth Lowman	I thank Thee, Lord, for life
1970–80	Mrs Joan Newland	O Jesus, I have promised

Offertory and Dedication

1981+	Miss Nicola Wright	And did those feet (Jerusalem)

Prayers and the Lord's Prayer

Hymn

Benediction

Organist   Mr David Old   LGSM

Excerpts from the Newsletter of June 1982

Few of us who were in church on the evening of 29 April will forget the delightful presentation of the 'History of Henleaze' by the children of Henleaze Junior School under the guidance of their teacher, Mrs Haddy. The drawings and writing were both entertaining and instructive and listening to the children's voices recording their compositions whilst viewing slides of their expeditions was a charming idea. Many hours of thought and work must have gone into the exhibition, and we are grateful to the school and to Mrs Haddy for such a notable contribution to our festivities.

Though in different mood, the barn dance was a great success, organised by leaders of the uniformed organisation, Junior Church, and Youth Group. It was a happy occasion which everyone, young and old obviously enjoyed. The age range very nearly spanned the life of the church! The large hall was filled to capacity with dancers, some more nimble-footed than others, but all entering the spirit of celebration aided by the music and direction of Peter Sumner and his Folk Companions.

Our 75th church anniversary Sunday was celebrated with great joy and thanksgiving for all the blessings of past years. The active participation of so many in the morning service demonstrated that we are truly a family church.

At the church tea-party, we welcomed twenty-five friends from Wrington and fifty-eight from Dursley along with friends from St Peter's and the Westbury Council of Churches.

The 'Songs of Praise' was a delight to us all and we are so grateful to all who took part, especially to Mr Harold Sylvester for his 'sympathetic interviewing', and to Mr David Old for his beautiful solo and organ accompaniments. It was a day of thanksgiving that we shall not easily forget.

Visit to Lee Abbey

The visit to Lee Abbey was part of our 75th Anniversary celebrations. A party of some 25 members, most of whom had not sampled the delights of Lee Abbey before went away for a weekend together. The countryside around was exceptionally beautiful, a backcloth for a weekend from which all gained so much. It was a wonderful chance for members of the church to get to know each other better. The tremendous warmth of fellowship, which permeated through the Lee Abbey Community, radiated throughout the whole weekend of discussion, worship, social gatherings and free time. People came away reluctantly and expressed the hope that there might be a repeat visit.

In 1982 the URC General Assembly was held in the Colston Hall. Members of Henleaze URC were involved with the provision of hospitality for the Representatives attending from URCs all over the country.

During Lent 1985 our children laid a trail of 1775 two-penny pieces in aid of famine relief in Ethiopia.

Abbeyfield

In the mid-70s the church was very actively involved through Sheila Llewellyn in the setting up of a new Abbeyfield Home for the elderly at 45 Westbury Road. The Home provides accommodation, meals and freedom from the worries and loneliness of living alone that some people experience. Sheila was voluntary House Manager on the House Committee once it was opened, a position she held until she retired through poor health. She was made an Honorary Vice President of the Abbeyfield Society in recognition of all her work. Another member, Jean Renshaw, received a certificate for 20 years service on the general committee.

Up until 1999 when the Abbeyfield Home in Westbury Road was reorganised, church members joined with other groups to cook lunch for the residents on the housekeeper's day off. Such was the fame of the dessert provided by one of our members that she was known as 'Mrs Trifle'.

Links are still maintained with Abbeyfield with gifts of flowers, donations and invitations to our social events.

Youth Club 1983–90

George and Nora Neilson wrote:

> We took over the running of the Henleaze URC Youth Group in 1983. The club represented a good mix of teenagers most of whom were associated with the church and part of the FURY group. We met every Thursday from 7.30 to 9.30pm in the Waterford Hall. Activities included table tennis, pool, five-a-side, badminton, snooker and a variety of other games. There were also 'fish and chips nights', visits to the ice-skating rink, bowling alleys and an annual weekend camp which invariably ended with us all soaked to the skin by rain.

Youth Club Camp

The club provided the young with a place to meet and chat with their friends and let off some steam. Several special events were organised, most memorable of which were three gigs – one performed by a well-known Christian rock group, Rebel X, and two performed by a group of home-grown talent. The funds raised in the latter two cases were donated to CLIC, a Bristol charity.

Most members attended our church and participated in various events organised by FURY, some of which included overnight stays at other churches in the Bristol area. In 1990 the club merged with the Junior Church and is now absorbed within FURY.

Junior Church

Ron and Mary Huish first became involved in Junior Church in 1972, and Don Kimber was recruited to take on the older age group which had to be split in two because of numbers. They started to use the storeroom in Church House which required redecorating, and asked the youngsters what colours they would like. They chose purple – if you look now you will see that the ceiling is still that colour! Around 1974 Ron Huish became Junior Church leader when numbers were in decline and recruitment of teachers was becoming increasingly difficult on account of the serious wider problems facing the church at that time.

During Ron Bocking's Ministry, the lesson material was changed to 'Partners in Learning', with structural training sessions for the leaders, prep class meetings etc. A real effort was made to plan services which would attract parents of Guides and Brownies who often attended the monthly 'parade' services. There was also greater involvement of Junior Church in, and during, the main worship.

Junior Church activities included rounders on the Downs (where the staff used to get trounced) with a picnic afterwards, summer coach outings, games and walks evenings for all ages, football against other church sides and on one occasion a trip to Blaise Park when three girls were lost for half an hour or so.

There was always a Junior Church Christmas party. One year, the party was described as follows:

> Sunday, January 12 in the Leonard Hall was a scene of conspicuous consumption, with 96 sausages in bread rolls liberally laced with tomato ketchup, fruit juice, crisps, iced buns, meringues etc. We were entertained by a clown – yes – a real clown, Wilbur the Great, dressed in baggy trousers, with a bright red nose (his own) and red bowler hat over his quite startling red hair. Wilbur not only mystified us by his tricks (with considerable audience participation) but cycled up and down the hall on a monocycle, juggling at the same time!

Brownies and Guides

By 1977 there were 42 Guides in the 44th Company and with several Brownies ready to go up to the Guides, it was decided to form a second company, the 21st. During this time a number of Guides achieved their Queen's Guide Award, the first being a daughter of a junior church leader.

Highlights in the Guides' life included the celebrations for the Guides Diamond Jubilee (1910–70) when they paraded along Anchor Road to Hotwells and Deanery Road where the Lord Mayor and city dignitaries took the salute, and when the Scarlet Pimpernel Patrol got into the finals of the Polycell Jubilee competition. This took them to Girl Guide head-quarters in London where they won third prize and £10 to be spent on equipment for their patrol.

Meanwhile the remainder of 44th Company were camping at Westonbirt, described by one under the heading 'Rain … rain … and more rain'.

During the 1980s the Brownie Pack continued to flourish, taking part in traditional events like 'Thinking Day', held each year on 22 February,

Queen's Guide Celebrations

when they remembered their founders and Brownies throughout the world. Locally, at Christmas time Brownies visited old people's homes singing carols. They worked for badges such as the challenge badge by helping the disabled and by raising money for charity. On another occasion they visited Southmead Police Station as part of the Crime prevention badge and saw how the breathalyser worked. They couldn't experience the cells because they were full of prisoners.

More recently, the 44th Henleaze Brownie Pack celebrated the award of the 20-year service badge to Sheila Budd, their Brown Owl, and wrote her an appreciative poem:

Thanks Brown Owl
Every Thursday without fail she gives a welcome greeting
To all the Henleaze Brownies for the 44th pack meeting
The church hall at the URC is like her second home
And where she's offered 'guidance' to the pixies, sprites, elves and gnomes
Encouraging us all she does, what more can Brownies ask?
She's always there to 'lend a hand' and help them with their task
She'll teach you to cook biscuits, make a bandage or a sling
She's there to cheer at Sports Day and to sing at Brownie Ring

She leads the troops at church parade and at St George's Day
And every year for one w/e she takes us all away
The Brownies love her stories, trails, night hikes and campfires best
They call it a pack holiday but she goes HOME for a rest
And so the time has come for her to fly to pastures new
What can we say but 'thanks Brown Owl good luck and we will miss you'

Mothers and Toddlers

Mothers and toddlers group first met in September 1980 on Wednesday afternoons. This began as a joint venture by our church and St Peter's. No such group existed before this. It became a project of Henleaze URC in May 1990. Jean Renshaw and Mary Huish ran it for 14 years, retiring in 2003, when it was taken over by Sue Wright and Diane Main. Generations of parents and toddlers have come along to this group and found a friendly welcome and the opportunity to meet others at the same stage of parenthood and childhood. To the present day, this group is well-supported by people from the local community and has been one way in which new families are introduced to the church.

Brownies' Christmas Coffee Morning

Crossroads

There were changes afoot towards the end of Ron Bocking's ministry. Services, after three years of discussion, were moved to the earlier start time of 10.30am. The church had started to talk about the building and suggestions about changing the back of the church, particularly the entrances, were beginning to take shape. They experimented with the building by 'turning it around' one Sunday, with the congregation sitting in the apse and the Minister standing near one of the pillars. They thought about creating a second storey of rooms within the back of the church building for meetings and the like. Redevelopment, or sale, of some of the Church House building was also considered.

In 1983 a group of church members was set up to consider Henleaze United Reformed Church's future. Their report together with the shortened version entitled 'Cross Roads' covered church life, involvement with other churches, finance and buildings.

It was felt that Sunday Services should begin at 10.30am or even earlier to allow time for 'gathering afterwards'. Services needed to be more 'joyful' with greater participation by Members and their families with 'chorus singing' and playing of musical instruments.

Church meetings needed to be held on a more regular basis – such as the first Thursday in the month and needed to have a 'more positive programme of topics'.

The growth of House Groups was welcomed, but it was felt that Elders needed to do more pastoral work, perhaps 'visiting in twos'. As for involvement with other churches, the links with St Peter's were good and should be extended. The authors of the report also wondered what the situation was at Trinity URC and whether there might be any interest in linking up permanently in the future.

Moving on to the church finances, the report expressed concern at the shortfall in giving, which represented 1% –2% of average net income. If the members could raise their giving to 5% not only would their problems disappear but they would also be able to increase their giving to outside causes. It was felt that there should be a drive to increase church membership and at the same time make members aware of the costs of running the church. So it was planned to issue 'The Simple Person's Guide to Church Running Costs'.

Closely linked to the financial problems was the state of the church buildings, it being calculated that some £40–£50,000 was needed for the maintenance of the buildings. Asking the question 'Are the premises the best possible to do the Lord's work in the years 1990–2000', they concluded the answer was probably 'no', due largely to the lack of proper maintenance and the prohibitive cost of heating the church 'for only about three hours per week'.

The report then proposed three alternatives for the future of the church buildings:-

1. Internal Alterations – making the building more viable disposing of the new hall, reassessing the use of the Leonard Hall building and 'possibly part could become the Manse'.
2. Complete redevelopment of the site – with multi-purpose buildings, incorporating elderly persons' flats on part of the site, resulting in greater involvement in Community work.
3. Development of site with community rooms etc, using St Peter's Church for services on a properly shared basis, but still maintaining our independence.

It was felt that the need to move forward was urgent and so the City Planning Department had been approached and indicated that it would be likely to approve the redevelopment of the church and its rooms with residential accommodation.

Opinion Survey – 1985

It may be of interest to see that in 1985 the congregation members were asked to consider these questions:

1. Which of the following statements do you think is nearer the truth.
   a) A Christian community can exist without a church building. (10%)
   b) A church building is an essential to the life of a Christian community. (90%)
2. Which of the following most nearly describes your views:
   a) Henleaze URC is an integral part of my life. (50%)
   b) I would miss very much not being able to go to Henleaze URC. (75%)
   c) I wouldn't feel happy going to any other church. (10%)
   d) If Henleaze URC was not there I would happily attend another church. (55%)
3. Which of the following do you think are true. I regard Henleaze URC as:
   a) An essential part of the Christian witness in Henleaze. (50%)
   b) An integral part of the community life of Henleaze. (50%)

c) The spiritual home of the members of the church and
congregation. (70%)
4. Select one of the following:
a) I don't see the merit of spending a lot of money on the church
buildings. (15%)
b) If the church buildings need maintenance we shall just
have to set about getting the money. (85%)
5. Do you agree (+) of disagree (-) with the following statements:
a) Henleaze URC does not pay enough attention to mission to non-
believers. (40%+/40%-)
b) Henleaze URC is too preoccupied with money and buildings.
(75%+/10%-)
c) Henleaze URC is more activity centred than God centred.
(65%+/10%-)
6. Which of the following do you think are true?
Henleaze URC would attract more new members if :
a) It had more facilities for young people. (40%)
b) It was more comfortable and better decorated. (20%)
c) It had more festival-type services. (38%)
d) More effort was made to evangelise the neighbourhood. (30%)

110 replies were received.

Church House and the caretaker's flat

The upper floor to Church House, the original building on the site, was
utilised as a residence for the church caretaker. In 1979, Mrs Stoodley
the caretaker, retired. Another couple arrived to take up the post and live
in the flat – but soon disappeared without warning, leaving no
forwarding address and several unpaid bills! After this, the church
reviewed its use of the flat and practice of employing caretakers. They
decided instead to offer the flat to married students training for the
Methodist church ministry at Wesley College, with the idea that the
student's spouse would act as caretaker and oversee the opening, closing
and security of the buildings. This arrangement proved to be mutually
beneficial and many good friendships were formed. Wesley College and
the church saw another opportunity in this arrangement and over the
years the student living in the caretaker's flat became formally 'on
placement' with the church. It grew into an opportunity for healthy
ecumenical cooperation.

In the later alterations to buildings, when these student and caretaker arrangements had ceased, the flat was converted into accommodation for the growing Junior Church.

Manses

Records show that in our 100-year history we have had four Manses, which in date order are:

4 Park Grove
35 Cavendish Road
30 Henleaze Park Drive
6 Owen Grove

Parallel Ordinations of Church of England and URC candidates for Ministry 1985

Henleaze URC was involved, in 1985, in an unique event. This was the 'parallel Ordination' of a number of URC and Church of England Ordinands who, having trained and studied together, expressed the wish to be ordained in the same ceremony.

This request raised several doctrinal problems for both denominations. Whilst at this time the URC ordained women as Ministers, the Church of England only allowed them ordination as Deacons. This practice in the Church of England had given rise to the Movement for the Ordination of Women, whose members interrupted ordination ceremonies with verbal protests and the distribution of leaflets. In addition, while Church of England candidates were ordained in their Cathedral Church, those of the URC were ordained in the church in which they were to serve.

Ron Bocking, as Chair of the Bristol District, played a major role in devising the Parallel Ordination. One of the two URC candidates for ordination was Mary Piggot (Basil Rogers was the other), and she not only agreed to be ordained in Bristol Cathedral alongside her Church of England colleagues, but also persuaded the Movement for the Ordination of Women to restrict their protest to distributing leaflets in silence.

The Parallel Ordination was held in a packed Bristol Cathedral before members of both the URC and the Church of England and was, in the words of Mary Piggot, a 'wonderful occasion'.

Ron Bocking said of the Parallel Ordinations that here is 'a sign of what is possible when people catch the vision and trust one another in seeking to discover where God is leading.'

Mary was appointed, by the Bristol District Council of the URC, to be Associate Minister at Redland Park, Henleaze and Horfield, whilst continuing to do her full time job. She took the service one Sunday a month in Henleaze where, during Ron Bocking's sabbatical she was appointed to pastoral oversight of the church.

CHAPTER 5

OUR CHURCH TODAY

1987–2007

Ministers:
Bernard Chart 1989–94
John Salsbury 1996–2001
Tracey Lewis 2003–

These years are within the memory of our present church members and friends. The Cold War came to an end but the world did not become a safer place due to the spread of international terrorism and conflict in the Middle East. At home, there was devolution for Scotland and Wales and the prospect of peace in Northern Ireland.

The Reverend Bernard Chart 1989–94

Despite the concern of the Elders expressed in the 1983 report on the future of the URC and in particular its buildings, the issues continued to be discussed for the remaining years of Revd. Ron Bocking's Ministry.

Each Elders' meeting, and church meetings too, were concerned with debating the proposals for updating church buildings, without reaching a final decision. Architects were consulted but still no decision was taken. Perhaps they could leave it until a new Minister replaced Ron Bocking, who retired in 1985, after all 'the quality of members was more important than luxurious buildings'.

Meanwhile the church was experiencing difficulties in finding a new Minister. Two prospective Ministers had turned down the offer and it was even suggested that Elders 'visit URC churches when on holiday to try to find a Minister for ourselves. Any negotiations would, of course, go through the Moderator'.

At this point Bernard Chart, Minister in an inner city Derby Church, was looking for a 'neighbourhood church' for the final years of his Ministry. He saw that Henleaze URC was in need of a Minister and approached the Moderator, who told him that 'Henleaze had problems'.

Bernard Chart

Undeterred by this, Bernard Chart was introduced to Henleaze and decided this was the church for him.

Bernard Chart's induction at Henleaze was attended by a coach load of members from his former Derby Church, who expressed surprise at his choice. 'Why have you come here?' they asked, 'it's such a miserable place!' Indeed, with the heavy wooden doors and thick curtains obscuring the interior of the church, it hardly offered worshippers a welcome.

Church redevelopment

Bernard knew that they needed to 'do something with the buildings' and the 1991 proposals for the future were prepared by a Sub-Committee:

1. That the buildings be brought up to standard to meet the new Hygiene Act and more attractive to tenants as an immediate temporary measure.
2. The Development Committee to look again at the Leonard Hall/Church House site and cost of refurbishment.
3. Long term plan to refurbish Church House.

Redevelopment of the church interior

The Development Group decided to go ahead and draw up a list of the necessary tasks in the kitchens and toilets to meet hygiene regulations stating 'we should do as much work as possible ourselves'.

A Church Redevelopment Fund was set up to which church members subscribed generously and a number of fund raising activities got under way. The first of which was a sponsored parachute jump in 1989. The jump was organised by Reg Isaacs, who had been a member of the Parachute Regiment during his service with the Armed Forces. Reg and three other church friends made the jump which raised the sum of £1200. It was ironical that whilst the inexperienced parachutists landed safely, Reg did not and fractured a bone in his foot.

The refurbishment of the church building took place in 1991 when about £150,000 was spent on general alterations including the replacement of the wooden doors with Derby glass, the addition of a dividing screen to form the meeting area at the rear of the church, re-arrangement of the entrances, the provision of a coffee bar, forming the quiet room and the raised dais at the front of the church at the chancel floor level, as well as considerable maintenance and repair work generally. At the same time, we were able to sand down and re-polish the wood block flooring throughout the church, which had an amazing effect on the

Reg Isaacs and Paul Morrow presenting the money raised by their parachute jump

general appearance of the building. The successful fund raising and the achievement of meeting our objective was mainly due to the enthusiasm and leadership of our minister at that time, the Revd. Bernard Chart. At the conclusion of this work much of the re-decorating work was done by church Members who felt that 'the decorating was something we could do ourselves' and a list of volunteers was drawn up of people willing to do small maintenance jobs. Paul Bloomfield will always be remembered for the enormous contribution he made to the care and maintenance of the church buildings during the refurbishment and beyond.

Friday Prayer Group

The Friday prayer group was started by Bernard Chart soon after the creation of the Quiet Room in 1990. Initially Bernard led prayers each week and one or two members of the group helped out when he wasn't available. Over the years Prayer Group meetings have been attended by some 30 or more people, many of whom have prepared and led prayers.

By 1993 there was a full rota, a quarterly communion service and, in August, meetings with morning coffee for prayer group members only. The following year the 'coffee morning' was opened up to all who came along on a Friday morning.

In the group, prayers are requested for church members, their families, and people known to be in stressful situations. The prayer requests are written in the Book of Intercessions. Members then lead the group in prayers, the reading of the Bible and the sharing of reflections or stories of people who have lived saintly lives. All who attend feel surrounded by friendship and fellowship.

A prayer, discovered in a book belonging to a faithful member of the group who has since died, sums up the thoughts and hopes of this Prayer Group:

Lord help me,
To take the time to stand in the shoes of the other person,
To start where they are,
To listen to what they feel,
To refrain from the too hasty judgement or the too ready answer,
To smile and be gentle,
And yet not to collude with the slipshod,
But prayerfully to see a thing through.

Bristol Child Contact Centre

The Bristol Child Contact Centre, known at first as the Access Centre, opened in November 1990 and with very few exceptions (when Christmas Day has fallen on a Saturday) has been available every week from 2 to 5pm, providing friendly neutral surroundings in which separated parents can meet with their children when all other means have been tried and failed. The centre came into being as a result of a Probation Family Court meeting when Evelyn Bentley, then a magistrate, heard of the desperate need for such a service. With the encouragement of Bernard Chart, the then Westbury Council of Churches was approached, the need for financial support and volunteers to man the centre being essential. Both were willingly offered, a committee was formed under the chairman-ship of Revd. Canon John Rogan, at that time Director of the Bristol Diocesan Board for Social Responsibility. More financial support was given by the Greater Bristol Trust with the intention of occupying church premises every Saturday afternoon it was essential that whichever church eventually provided the necessary accommodation for the centre should not suffer financially. Our own Leonard Hall was eventually chosen for safety reasons with the added blessing that the playgroup, already in existence, was willing to allow the use of their equipment until the centre was in a more secure financial position. It was several years later before a financial arrangement was agreed by the Probation Service. In the interim the centre received generous financial help from many sources and individuals, the churches in the Westbury area, the Bristol Solicitors' Family Law Association and a choir conducted by Peter Wilkinson, a Bristol solicitor, which gave concerts in our church, making it possible to buy equipment and the large cupboard in the Leonard Hall to accommodate it.

There was a limit to the number of children who could be accommodated each week and requests showed no signs of decreasing so, with the help of church friends in South Bristol and the support of the National Association of Child Contact Centres, now in being, to which the Bristol Centre was affiliated, a new centre was opened in a church building in Bedminster. This has been a great help to the families living in South Bristol.

The centre is a child-centred project; any work with the parents is to ensure that the contact process is of the highest quality for the child. A Contact Centre is not a crèche, nor a child-minding service, its sole objective is to provide a neutral, non-threatening, warm and caring environment where children can meet their non-custodial parent.

It is a sad commentary on the failed relationships within our society that the need for the centre (and the many others which are now established) shows no sign of diminishing.

'NEW LIFE' Sunday 29 April 1989

The New Life Sunday was a very special day for many young people in all of the nine member churches of the Westbury Council of Churches. On the Sunday evening the Westbury Council United Service was held in this church. The theme of the service was 'New Life' and the young people, mainly of junior school age had enthusiastically rehearsed hymns which they sang with special accompaniment. In addition there was some choral speaking, music and movement. The earlier time of 6.00 pm had been arranged so that younger children could be present. Parents were encouraged to support the young people's endeavours and to participate in this united act of worship.

One young reader had to be given a stool to stand on. Some girls had learnt a ballet to the Lord's Prayer. The service was well supported by parents – they were queuing out of the church– and the offering was substantial – and resulted in The Westbury Council of Churches having some funds. Soon after the Contact Centre was started – and the churches were able to give £500 for the beginning of the Contact Centre.

Junior Church 1992–2003

In 1992 Julie Morrow took over the role of Junior Church Co-ordinator from Evelyn Bentley. We had a thriving Primary department, a large 7–10 year old group, and we could see the need to divide the rest of our young people into two further groups. Space was becoming a problem. We set about converting the old caretaker's flat above Church House, which gave us three new teaching rooms and a much needed resource base. Teachers and children helped with the decorating and we even had carpets – bright emerald green – remnants from an indoor bowling green! At last, Junior Church had a permanent home where the children's work could be displayed and projects left out from one Sunday to the next.

At staff meetings there were endless debates on which teaching resources to use but, whether we continued to use *Partners in Learning* or swapped to *Scripture Union*, Sunday mornings were always a hive of activity. Bible stories were read, acted, mimed, even sung. Games and quizzes were popular and, in true 'Blue Peter' style, we cut, stuck and painted to reinforce the message. It was a time of picnics in the park, of rounders on the Downs, traditional Christmas parties and visits to the pantomime.

In the wider context, our young people were offered more opportunities to explore their faith through activities beyond Junior Church. The Music Group was formed, which proved to be of fundamental importance in retaining the interest of many teenagers, as did the inter-church football tournaments in which our teams won a fair number of trophies. The Crasis youth group met in Alison Rugg's house every other Sunday evening and residential events at Yardley Hastings, the URC National Resource Centre, were well attended. All of these were opportunities for our young people to introduce their non-church friends and to network with other young Christians across the country. For the first time in many years, a group of our teenagers wanted to explore their faith and commitment, leading to their confirmation and church membership.

Towards the end of 1998, the Junior Church coordinator drew up a list of all the things she did in that role. It included everything from chairing business meetings to writing birthday cards for every child on role (50+). No wonder it took best part of a year to find someone to take over! Her successor reduced the list to six key items, 'volunteering' other teachers to

The caretaker's flat undergoing conversion to Junior Church rooms

take on the rest of the tasks. During John Salsbury's ministry, and the following interregnum, our monthly planning meetings were led by Don Kimber. He skilfully guided and encouraged two dedicated teams of teachers, welcoming two new staff at our union with Trinity Church in 2002.

In an attempt to follow the 'Five Marks of Mission' our business meetings adopted a five part agenda. Teach (an obvious item), transform (here, we debated such things as the URC Good Practice document), tend (our response to human need featured highly in the Treasurer's report), tell (newsletter contributions and family services came into this category) and treasure (our resources). As a result of this focus, we developed our first mission statement:

To provide a place, within the overall church, for young people to receive religious education, guidance and support as they start their journey to discover their own Christian faith.

Junior Church had become increasingly involved in family services but it was during the inter-regnum that we planned and led them more or less on a monthly basis. New hymns and worship songs became a regular feature, many being introduced by the young people themselves from their experiences at Yardley Hastings, Spring Harvest, and Soul Survivor. The Christmas Eve teatime service, started in the late 1980s by Bernard Chart, had evolved from a straightforward re-telling of the nativity story into a major production. With the help of the Music Group, we had staged the play *Michael Mouse*, performed numerous sketches including one written by two of our own young people and, in 2003, put on the musical *Hosanna Rock*.

Junior Church leaders discovered that teaching and learning is a two-way process and it is a privilege to share in youthful vision which makes its impact on the journey of faith for all. The final song in *Hosanna Rock* expresses something young people are passionate about:

'Work for justice and for peace … for in Jesus's name we stand!'

The present day Junior Church

Chris Hyland writes:
Trinity-Henleaze has a large, vibrant Junior Church comprising of approximately fifty children and young people, supported by seventeen teaching staff.

The children and young people range from the age of three until sixteen, although they are welcome to continue after that age if they want to. They are divided into four classes, following mainly 'key stage' school groups.

Christmas Eve Nativity Service

Junior Church picnic

The teaching staff are divided into two teams, teaching alternative months using Scripture Union teaching aids. We also have a team of assistants, who help when necessary. Teaching takes many different forms, hopefully making it lively and interesting for everyone.

We encourage the children and young people to join the main body of the church whenever possible. We participate with the monthly all-age worship and have several members in the Music Group. Other activities include holding an Easter sale and organising and running the (by now) annual Easter breakfast. At Christmas we participate in the Christmas Eve service, and try to organise a trip or a party at this time for all ages. In July, we hold a summer picnic to which the whole church are invited. We help with the Remembrance Day service. Crasis takes place fortnightly during term times, where senior school children and young people meet to discuss topics and have various activities.

The Junior Church is a vital part of the future of the church. Recently, we have had several baptisms, some of children whose first contact with the church came through the Mums and Tots group, we hope that when they are old enough the children will join us in the Junior Church. At the other end of the spectrum five young people have been confirmed into the membership of the church. Hopefully, this will be an on-going process, enabling our church to continue for successive generations.

Crasis

Alison Rugg has run the youth group, Crasis, since its inception.

In 1990 there were few activities for the teenagers apart from the Junior Church, uniformed organisations, and the badminton club. In order to provide an evening activity, where these young people could meet with their peer group within the church, it was decided to join with Redland Park URC's youth group for a year. So, the leader and three young people from Henleaze met at Redland Park fortnightly from 7.15pm until 9.15pm. This was so successful that eventually numbers became too large (17+ from both churches) that each church decided to run its own group.

The name Crasis was chosen by the young people, being a Greek word meaning 'everybody coming together.'

Aims of the Crasis Group

To bring the young people of Trinity-Henleaze United Reformed Church to Christianity.

Crasis has similar aims to that of the youth organisation of the United Reformed Church FURY, which aims to provide fun, faith and fellowship to all young people who are linked in any way to the United Reformed Church. Crasis aims to do this locally in Henleaze.

Crasis is an open and inclusive group and the young people are encouraged to bring their friends. The activities are determined by:

Crasis group

1. Listening to the ideas of the young people.
2. Fitting in with the needs of the church and its other organisations.
3. Becoming involved, wherever practical, in Christian events arranged by other URC youth bodies and other Bristol churches.

Objectives

1. To meet on a regular basis on a Sunday evening (once per fortnight in term time).
2. To do fun activities.
3. To attend Christian events aimed at young people.
4. To raise money for charity.
5. To support other activities organised by the church.
6. To create a critical mass of young people of Trinity Henleaze URC who 'belong' to each other and the church and share similar beliefs and faith.
7. To inject additional Christian teaching to the group and bring young people to church membership.

The programme is a mixture of events, generally including active sessions with food. The group enjoys ten-pin bowling, board games, arts and crafts, annual visit to the fireworks, the occasional Chinese takeaway, a game of rounders on the Downs, Ready Steady Cook evenings and much more. There are not many evening outings that cost money but weekends away are popular.

Since Crasis was formed the numbers of young people at the church has risen. There are now about 21 aged between 12 and 17. Five young people became church members in September 2006 and another four are currently attending the Membership class.

Music – from Bach to barn dances

The organ

In 1992 the family of the late Norah Jewell, as a memorial to her contribution to church music, gave a tonally superior stopped diapason rank to replace the great clarabella within the organ.

In three stages during 1996 and 1997, through the initiative of John Bishop (our organist 1974–76) and with advice from the organ builder Tony Cawston, the Haskins organ was provided with an adjustable bench, re-tuned to concert pitch to match that of the new piano and extended to a significant degree. The aim of the extension was to widen the organ's tonal palette, whilst retaining its historic character, so as to enhance its suitability for recital and concert use. This was achieved by adding a mixture, a fifteenth and a reed (trumpet) rank to the great, replacing the swell reed with a closed horn and adding a 16ft reed to augment the pedal. The dummy display pipes on the outside of the organ case were then re-gilded. The cost of all this work was met by donations from two of our church members.

John Bishop first demonstrated the organ's new capacity in a recital after its second rededication.

The church has contributed in many ways to the wider musical world, particularly in our neighbourhood and city. The archives refer to many special occasions. For example broadcast services for 'Sunday Half Hour', 'Songs of Praise' and a Christmas morning service for the BBC in which the congregation experienced a live link with a church in Jerusalem, and the Bristol Hymn Festival of September 1997. Alan Bull's 'Songs of Praise and Hymns of Prayer' was a memorable musical event during the ministerial interregnum of 2001, recorded to mark Bert Bentley's retirement as organist. We also remember the recording, in aid of church funds, of 'Music at Henleaze' by John Bishop and his friends. Notable

The piano presented by Marianne Parry

Music Group

during the pastorate of Revd. John Salsbury was the staging in church in 1998 of a sacred musical drama in the modern idiom, *The Singing Dancing Carpenter* to which reference is made elsewhere.

In 1992 Marianne Parry gave the church a Yamaha conservatoire grand piano as a memorial to her long-time friend Shirley Jones. This generous act awakened an interest in our church building as an ideal small centre for the professional performing arts that continues to this day. We now had a piano to suit a virtuoso, a fine acoustic, comfortable seating (thanks to the late Audrey Venning in funding the replacement of our aging chairs with a comfortable upholstered alternative) and, as a result of the imaginative changes to the layout of the chancel in 1994, ample platform space for an orchestra. Our connection with Roger Huckle and the Emerald Ensemble led at first to a series of concerts devoted to the music of J S Bach. This was followed, on the initiative of Revd. Bernard Chart, by the formation in 1994 of the Henleaze Concert Society, with Bernard as its first chairman, which continues to offer a series of six concerts by professional musicians that regularly play to full houses in our church each year. In these years John Bishop and his friends gave many memorable concerts in aid of church funds using the new piano and the re-voiced organ, including a series to celebrate a joint anniversary in 1997 of Brahms, Mendelssohn and Schubert.

The most important role for music in our church life is, of course, the part it can play in divine worship Sunday by Sunday. And in this we have been blessed in recent times by the revival of an old tradition in congregational worship, that of the church band, in the shape of our Music Group led by Lee Budd and John Searle. Here we have a talented all-age group of instrumentalists – piano with strings, brass, woodwind and percussion – who regularly provide the accompaniment for hymns and songs at morning worship in a style that sets the feet tapping.

We value the contribution that the Singing Group makes to Sunday morning worship at festival times. And barn dances and cabaret in the Waterford Hall feature regularly when our church family enjoys letting its hair down.

The Reverend John Salsbury 1996–2001

Henleaze URC was John Salsbury's final Ministry before he retired and in his own words was 'a marvellous way to end'. (All the last three Ministers had gone on to retirement.) His Ministry has been referred to as 'the quiet

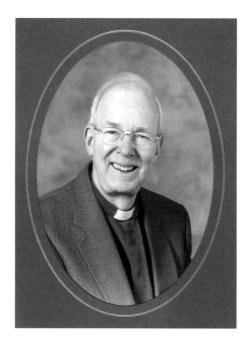

John Salsbury

Ministry' after the turmoil of rebuilding the congregation and restoring the church buildings. He believed that the church should be inclusive, open to all kinds of people and that everyone was on a lifelong journey for which they needed help along the way.

To this end, he reintroduced a Confirmation Class, 'I thought we had stopped doing that,' was a remark heard, and a Bible Study Meeting of some eight to ten people. A popular innovation in 1996 was the 'Advent Anthology' containing thoughts and prayers put together to 'help us in one preparation and celebration of Christmas'. The collection covered the period from Advent Sunday to Epiphany and some 37 church members shared their thoughts on the Scripture passages belonging to that season.

Worship at this time included the young people's Music Group as a regular feature of the monthly family service and a monthly evening service of a reflective nature attracted some 10–12 'faithful attendees'.

John Salsbury also felt that the social life of the church was important in providing opportunities to inter-connect and enjoy ourselves together. Perhaps the most outstanding example of this was his encouragement of *The Singing Dancing Carpenter* in 1998. It had been performed in his previous church and involved a great many church members. This ambitious musical revolved around some of the highlights of the Life and Teachings of our Lord and was told with song, dance and humour. It was

The Singing Dancing Carpenter

produced by Beryl Davey and her daughter Philippa Ross-Duffy. There were two performances at Henleaze URC and the production was taken round a number of other churches.

A newsletter article of the time reflected:

> We shared, among others, the pleasures of the wedding guests, the amazement of the repentant Zaccheus at his salvation and the fury of the wily conspirators... The work compelled us to ask ourselves what would have been our own reaction had we been invited to cast the first stone. We joyfully joined in the 'cry hosanna'. If we had been there, would we have joined with equal enthusiasm in the cry 'crucify Him'? For this reviewer the poignancy of the human predicament struck home most forcibly in the portrayal of Peter's agonised denial. And so to the final uplifting, joyful choruses. It was great!

John Salsbury retired in 2001 much appreciated for his teaching and his skill in bringing people together. In the words of a church member, 'he didn't push, he didn't go out in front but he sat in the midst of them'.

Ron Bocking, Bernard Chart and John Salsbury

The Walking Group

In 1999 a group of walkers and dogs, numbering up to 30 some days, set out to walk the Cotswold Way in several stages. They met fortnightly on Saturdays and drove from the church to their starting point in convoy. Walking together proved to be a great opportunity for conversation and the furthering of friendships. Half of the walkers were church members, the others being friends who called themselves 'social members'. The Cotswold Way, its total of 104 miles, provided marvellous scenery and good pubs along the way for lunch. Its completion brought a great sense of achievement for the walkers who had all had a lot of fun.

In 2000 the walkers ventured out along the Limestone Link and the Mendip Way. 2001 and 2002 saw two walking weekends based at the Swanage Youth Hostel – the first of these trips being famous for the walk along Studland Beach into a brisk April wind, when the group discovered the extreme hardiness of the local nudists.

In subsequent years the walkers did some of the Wye Valley walks and a shortened form of the Frome Valley Walkway.

The Walking Group

Uniting churches to become Trinity–Henleaze URC

In 2002 Henleaze URC was approached by Trinity URC, the former Presbyterian Church, Cranbrook Road, with a request that the two congregations begin a discussion about the possibility of uniting. Both churches were in a time of ministerial vacancy and considering their future direction. The elders of the two churches met, with the respective Interim Moderators, and discussed the proposal that the Trinity congregation would vacate their building and a new united church would come into being in the Henleaze building. After much debate it was decided to call the new congregation 'Trinity–Henleaze United Reformed Church.' The new congregation was commissioned to its life and mission together on 13 October 2002.

Extract from Newsletter, February 2004

Gordon Inglis writes for publication in *Reform:*

'Who's afraid of uniting?'

Trinity URC Bristol and Henleaze URC Bristol united to form Trinity-Henleaze URC on 13 October 2002. This uniting of two congregations, and the consequent release of one set of buildings was not as a result of District instruction, but a coming together of two congregations, both of which felt that union would strengthen them and enable money, which would have been spent on maintaining a large building, to be used for the benefit of the wider church.

Both churches were in a vacancy. Trinity members in considering their future, through careful prayer and deliberations in Elders' meetings and church meetings, felt the time was right to look outside their own church for a way forward. Having considered two other nearby URC churches, they felt an approach to Henleaze should take place. The main reason was that they discovered that 46% of their members lived within a mile of Henleaze URC – a higher percentage than lived within a mile of Trinity!

The first approach came as a complete surprise to Henleaze. A small committee from each church met and discussed the possibility of union. Comparisons between worship styles, frequency of meetings, methods of administration and many other matters showed that both churches were very similar. If the union was to go ahead, it was obvious that each congregation would have to accept some changes. However, the relations between the two groups were so positive that everyone, assisted by the two interim Moderators, felt that there was great merit in putting the proposal to the congregations.

Once the matter had been discussed and approved at the church meetings, a joint service was held at the Henleaze premises. The Trinity members were so warmly welcomed that any doubts were quickly dispelled. More than 75% of Trinity members and adherents indicated their wish to be part of the new church. This response was very gratifying to those most involved in the negotiations. The District Council was approached and approval of the formation of the new church Trinity-Henleaze URC was given.

The first service took place on 13 October 2002 and was followed on 19 October by a social evening to enable us all to get to know each other a little better. Members from both congregations are involved in the Elders and take part in the services. Efforts are being made to take the best procedures from each congregation's practice to ensure the smooth integration and strengthen the new church. We hope that in the near future we will find a new Minister to guide and lead us forward to achieve all we hope for through this union.

In these days, of heavy building maintenance costs, dwindling congregations and, worst of all a falling number of ministers, perhaps more churches should be forward looking and consider similar action – before it is forced upon them. It is not as painful or difficult as you may think. All that is needed is a willingness to look forward and to try to ascertain, through prayer, God's word to us.

The naming of the new united church caused much debate among the members. After consideration it was decided to name 'the belief first followed by the district', so the church became known as Trinity-Henleaze URC.

The Reverend Tracey Lewis 2003–

In the year following the union of the two congregations, the new church took great care to provide social opportunities for members to get to know one another and grow in friendship. The other pressing task before the fledgling Trinity-Henleaze URC was the search for a new minister. It was in the spring of 2003 that the Moderator introduced Tracey Lewis as a possible candidate. An appointments committee, consisting of members of both former congregations, conducted the initial interview, and by the early summer the call to be the Minister at Trinity-Henleaze URC had been issued and accepted.

Tracey Lewis

It was felt to be an exciting time in the life of the church as the union had opened opportunities for re-thinking the 'usual' patterns of church life. Appointing Tracey to be their minister, the congregation welcomed its first full time woman minister, who, returning to ministry after a seven and a half year break, brought a family with two young children to the Manse.

Connect 2003 and 2005

Churches Together in the Westbury Area (CTWA) provides a healthy meeting place and forum for cooperation between the churches of various denominations in Henleaze, Westbury Park, Stoke Bishop and Westbury on Trym. In both 2003 and 2005 the churches worked together to hold a fortnight of Arts, in the broadest sense, locally. There were concerts, drama, quizzes, fun days, children's activities, recitals and talks. Each church organised events which were coordinated and advertised together. The central weekend of the Connect fortnight saw an Arts Trail during which all of the churches were open with activities going on and exhibitions of paintings, textile art, pottery, calligraphy, flowers, and sculpture. People were invited to visit as many as they pleased.

In the Connect 2005 Festival, called 'Art and Soul', Trinity-Henleaze URC hosted a performance of the *Street Bible – Genesis to Revelation in 75 minutes!* by the Lacey Theatre Company. The Arts Trail saw the beginning of the patchwork wall hanging 'Let your light shine' that now hangs on the wall near the exits of the church. Members from all the CTWA churches, visitors to the exhibition from the local community, members and friends of the congregation from far and wide, Brownies and Junior Church were invited to embroider a small coloured square, including a cross in their design, to contribute to the whole work of some 380 squares. The wall hanging was completed, framed and hung by the autumn of 2006. It was dedicated at the harvest festival service.

Charitable Giving

A retiring collection is taken on the first Sunday of each month for a specific charity selected from among suggestions made by church members.

'Commitment for Life' features largely in the list and the money collected is divided between Christian Aid (75%) and the World Development Movement (15%) with 10% going to the URC for Mission Work.

In particular, local charities are supported and these have included the Jessie May Trust, Caring at Christmas, the Emmaus Project (work with the homeless) Kinergy, Children's Hospice South West and the Multiple Sclerosis Daystar Appeal.

Overseas charities have included Water Aid which works with some of the poorest people in the Third World to achieve real cost effective improvements in water supply, sanitation and hygiene. Phakamisa is a South African children's charity brought to our notice by church members, as was the needs of the church in East Timor. A talk by the brother of a church member, who had worked in East Timor, spoke of the struggles of the young nation and of the churches there. Told of the musical group in one church, who owned no instruments of their own, and had to borrow them, a church member was inspired to offer his instrument and funding to provide additional musical instruments was provided. The work in East Timor was supported for some three years.

There is always a huge need for charitable giving and suggestions for the names of additional charities are always welcome.

Outreach

The outreach work of the church is often thought of in terms of the activities promoted by the church as a whole. However, there are many individual church members who regularly give of their time and energy voluntarily to help 'good causes' within the city. Some work in charity shops (St Peter's Hospice, Tenovus for example) others as Co-ordinators of Neighbourhood Watch Schemes, and on local committees of the National Trust and One Step dance club for widows and widowers. They are to be found in the ranks of the Lions, and Rotary organisations which both raise money for charities and choral societies who support different good causes from the proceeds of their concerts. A less well-known charity supported by two of our members is the Caleb Bailey Charity supporting members of Baptist, Congregational and URC who preach or are studying to preach in congregations of these denominations.

Several church members have served as magistrates and school governors, organisers of the Contact and Access Centre and as secretary to a local Credit Union.

Other practical help is given by members in the Contact Centre, Home Farm Trust, the crèche at Horfield Prison, the coffee shop at the oncology centre, visiting victims of crime, counselling children and young people, listening to young readers in schools, voluntary driving for a GP's surgery, Meals on Wheels and food for the night shelter.

This is a mere snapshot of the many and varied activities in which church members are involved, showing their concern for the more vulnerable members of the community.

The social committee

A Church Social Committee was formed to bring everyone together whatever their age, to relax, be entertained and have fun and friendship. It also aimed to invite the community to share events with us, expanding our outreach as a church and to help increase the success of our fundraising groups.

The committee began with six people, increased to eight and is able to call on the services of several other church members as and when required. Events held so far include: Harvest Lunches, a Traidcraft Fashion Show, Christmas Fair, an evening of 'Wine, Cuisine and Cabaret', a concert by the New Harmony Ladies Choir, Family Fun Quiz Night, a Book Sale, Magic Lantern Show and a Barn Dance.

In 2004 the first 'After Christmas Lunch' was held in the Waterford Hall in the week between Christmas and New Year. People from the local community who were alone over the Christmas period, were invited to come along for lunch and good company. The first year some 54 people came, by 2006 this number had risen to 90.

The committee not only arranges events but supports others who wish to do so, and will be much involved with the Centenary Celebrations throughout 2007.

For the future it is planned to put aside a regular morning or afternoon meeting place for all ages to share popular activities including cards and scrabble, and enjoy refreshments, occasional lunches and outings.

Traidcraft

Following discussions over an 18-month period, in which reservations were expressed concerning Sunday trading, Anna Holm's persistence prevailed and the first Traidcraft stall opened on 31st January 1999. The stall is held monthly, usually after the family service, and from its small beginnings has grown both in the quantity and range of goods sold, and its contribution to the social life of the church. The Fashion Show Day held on 18th June 2005, during the 'Make Poverty History' campaign, and the decision to become a Fair Trade Church, are highlights of this short history.

It is proposed to include a Traidcraft shop in the new development of the church buildings which will secure its future.

Changes in church meeting style

The church meeting is the regular gathering where church members think, discuss and decide upon the priorities and direction of church life together. The church meetings were held in a formal business-like style, with which some people felt a measure of frustration. So, after discussion, it was agreed that we needed to encourage a wider range of people from the con-gregation to attend and take part in church meetings, and to do this we needed to vary the way we meet. In 2005/6 we began to experiment by holding some church meetings on a Sunday over a simple lunch of soup and bread, including children and young people and hence enabling their parents to attend, encouraging discussion by having small groups gathered around different subjects of which people could choose according to their interest. These changes saw an increasing involvement in the discussions at the heart of church life, and the emergence of interest or tasks groups. The 'Eco Group', which encourages the congregation to grow in its awareness of the environment and take action to protect it, was initiated by a discussion at one of these Sunday church meetings.

The 'Month of Sundays'

In 2004 and 2005 the church encouraged participation in worship with a project called a 'Month of Sundays'. October was chosen as the month when the themes for our services would be taken from questions which the congregation were invited to submit. Questions were written and posted in a collection box during the months of June and July, they were advertised in the newsletter in September and then on Wednesdays in October people were invited to the Manse to discuss the questions in preparation for Sunday services. Questions asked included: How can a God of love allow suffering? What difference does prayer make in our lives and the world? How are Christians to live and share the gospel in a multi-cultural society? Which came first – Adam and Eve or evolution? Small groups of people gathered for the discussions and the subsequent worship was greatly enriched by the participation and debate.

This is one of several ways in which the church has explored worship. Encouraging the participation of people of all ages in the preparation of worship has opened up new possibilities and ways of thinking of and expressing the faith we hold together.

Henleaze @ Heart

The union of the two congregations in 2002, in the Henleaze building, meant that the Trinity URC building was sold for re-development as residential units. It became clear to Trinity-Henleaze URC, that within the structures and rules of the URC trustees, some of the resources released by this sale could be made available to the new church for capital building works should they be required.

In 2004 a group of church members with experience of buildings was convened by the church meeting to consider the three church and community buildings in our care. This group reported that while the church building was in good condition, the buildings used by the local community throughout the week were in need of attention. The Waterford Hall, particularly, was of growing concern. The community buildings are regularly used by a wide range of organisations including the Henleaze Garden Club, Jack in the Box children's gym and exercise classes, flower arrangers, Scottish dancers, exercise and relaxation classes and many others. The facilities were in need of modernising, including the provision of disabled access.

After considerable thought and debate throughout the congregation, it was decided to take the opportunity that the financial resources released by the union of the two churches offered us, to renew and redevelop the buildings in our care.

Wide-ranging discussions about the place of the church in the local community, the purpose and hopes of the church and community for partnership now and in the future and our sense of wanting to offer a warm and welcoming gathering place for the enrichment of life in our neighbourhood, were held. From all of this and conversations with some of our neighbours, the 'Henleaze @ Heart' project took shape.

Our plans for the buildings aim to provide open, welcoming, accessible rooms, halls and meeting places for the people of our church and community. The improved facilities, built to be both a beautiful addition to the neighbourhood and ecologically advanced for the preservation of the environment, aim to offer good quality space for gathering, furthering friendships and developing the sense of community in Henleaze. The project involves the demolition of the Waterford Hall, and its replacement with a new hall, annexed to the church by new link rooms, and an attractive walkway between the church and Leonard Hall and Church House which opens up a new 'face' onto the Henleaze Road side of our church.

Some of the stones, salvaged from the work of the developer on the Trinity URC building in Cranbrook Road, will be built into the new buildings, providing a link with the two strands of our history, woven into these new opportunities.

In January 2007, the dawn of our centenary year, we were granted planning permission for these developments by the Bristol City Council. The 'adventure' of additional fund-raising lies ahead of us.

Un-sung Heroes

In every church there are men and women who quietly and voluntarily carry out the many tasks which make for its smooth running. Trinity-Henleaze URC is no exception.

There are secretaries and treasurers, those who organise rotas for door stewards and for coffee on Fridays and Sundays, for the crèche, leaders of

Crasis and Junior Church, editors of the newsletter, convenors of the Telephone Prayer Fellowship and House Groups, chair of the Ladies Guild, conductors of music and singing groups, operators of the sound system, arrangers of church flowers and their distribution and supervisors of house to house collections (Christian Aid). Most of these people are well known but less visible are the organisers of church and hall lettings (ensuring valuable income for the church), and representatives on wider church bodies such as the South West Synod, Bristol District Council, Women's World Day of Prayer and CTWA.

But how many people know that one church member is responsible for the safe keeping of all the keys, or another for checking First Aid boxes, whilst also collecting Smartie tubes full of coins for Africa?

Over and above this are several church members who have made it their job, for many years, to care for the church fabric. They make up notice boards, check the lighting, the boiler and the heating system, and generally oversee the maintenance of the building. To this end one member gets to church each Sunday morning at 7.30am to check the heating (at 6am recently during problems with the boiler), and one of the ladies has for many years taken home the tea-towels for washing after Sunday coffee.

Many of the church members help with social functions and with outreach. Trinity-Henleaze URC owes a great debt of gratitude to all these people who are, each and every one of them, 'un-sung heroes.'

EPILOGUE

Recollections such as these bring memories of the men and women, who have given so much of their lives in service to God within our fellowship. As one generation succeeds another it is inevitable that some names are remembered only by a few, and especially by those who cherish their memory most dearly, others are forgotten. But no passage of time can reduce our indebtedness to them. We look to the future with hope and with a deep sense of gratitude, summed up in the words of a sonnet by Henry Compton.

Immortality

These fields, which now lie smiling in the sun
Were tamed and schooled to harvest long ago
By men, whose lives, whose names we cannot know
Who went, in silence, when their work was done.
Their furrows slowly traced, their crops, hard won
Have vanished like some ancient winter's snow,
Their hearts dispersed in dust, have ceased to glow,
Mere random bones declare their race is run.
And yet within the fields there lie in wait
Strange virtues, which to them, not to us belong,
And as we plod behind the plough
Which bares the gracious earth they wooed,
We know the strong compulsion laid by them on all their heirs
And cannot choose but plough our furrows straight.